D0567335

follower

BECOMING MORE THAN JUST A FAN OF JESUS

kyle idleman

ZONDERVAN®

ZONDERVAN

Follower

Derived from material previously published in Not a Fan.
Abridged by Kyle Idleman.

Requests for information should be addressed to:
Zondervan, *3900 Sparks Dr. SE, Grand Rapids, Michigan 49546*

ISBN 978-0-310-10808-5 (hardcover)
ISBN 978-0-310-10824-5 (ebook)

Cover design: Jamie DeBruyn
Interior design: Emily Ghattas

Printed in the United States of America

20 21 22 23 24 25 26 27 28 29 / LSC / 10 9 8 7 6 5 4 3 2 1

To my dad

Following you taught me to follow Jesus

Contents

Introduction

D.T.R.

Some of you will recognize what the letters D.T.R. stand for. If you're not sure, let me give you a hint. For a young man involved in a romantic relationship, these letters can be enough to strike fear into his heart. He likely dreads the D.T.R. talk. In fact, many young men will postpone, run away from, and put off the D.T.R. talk for as long as possible. I have even known a few guys who have terminated the relationship when they sensed that the D.T.R. talk was imminent.

Now do you want to guess what D.T.R. stands for?

Define the relationship.

This is the official talk that takes place at some point in a romantic relationship to determine the level of commitment. You want to see where things stand and find out if what you have is real.

In high school I went out on a first date with a girl that I really didn't know very well. We sat down in a booth at a restaurant and began the awkward first date conversation. During the appetizer I learned a little bit about her family. While we enjoyed the main course, she told me about her favorite movie. And then it happened. While we were eating our dessert she asked me, and I quote: *"Where do you see this relationship going?"* On the very first date she was trying to have the D.T.R. talk. I got out of there P.D.Q. That was the first and the last date.

I wasn't ready for that moment, but there comes a time when you need to define the relationship. It can be awkward. It can be uncomfortable. But eventually every healthy relationship reaches a point when the D.T.R. talk is needed. Is it casual, or is it committed? Have things moved past infatuation and admiration and towards deeper devotion and dedication? You need to intentionally evaluate the state of the relationship and your level of commitment to the person.

So here's what I want to ask you to do. In your mind picture yourself walking into a local coffee shop. You grab a snack and get a drink and then walk towards the back where it isn't crowded, and you find a seat at a small table. You take a sip of your drink and enjoy a few quiet minutes. Now, imagine that

Jesus comes in and sits down next to you. You know it's him because of the blue sash. You're unsure what to say. In an awkward moment you try to break the silence by asking him to turn your drink into wine. He gives you the same look he used to give Peter. Before he has a chance to respond, you suddenly realize you haven't prayed for your food. You decide to say your prayer out loud, hoping that Jesus will be impressed. You start off okay, but understandably you get nervous and pray "Three things we pray: to love thee more dearly, to see thee more clearly, to follow thee more nearly, day, by day, by day." You quickly say "Amen" when you realize you're quoting Ben Stiller's prayer from *Meet the Parents*.

Before you have a chance to make things more awkward, Jesus skips past the small talk and gets right to the point. He looks you in the eye and says, "It's time we define this relationship." He wants to know how you feel about him. Is your relationship with Jesus exclusive? Is it just a casual weekend thing, or has it moved past that? How would your relationship with him be defined? What exactly is your level of commitment?

Whether you've called yourself a Christian since childhood, or all of this is new to you, Jesus would clearly define what kind of relationship he wants to have with you. He wouldn't sugarcoat it or dress it up. He would tell you exactly what it means to follow him. As you're sitting in that coffee shop listening to Jesus give you the unedited version of what kind of relationship he wants with you, I can't help but wonder if the question, "Are you a follower of Jesus?" would be a challenging one to answer.

It may seem that there are many followers of Jesus, but if they were to honestly define the relationship they have with him, I am not sure it would be accurate to describe them as followers. It seems to me that there is a more suitable word to describe them. They are not *followers* of Jesus. They are *fans* of Jesus.

Here is the most basic definition of fan in the dictionary: *an enthusiastic admirer.*

It's the guy who goes to the football game with no shirt and a painted chest. He sits in the stands and cheers for his team. He's got a signed jersey hanging on his wall at home and multiple bumper stickers on the back of his car. But he's never in the game. He never breaks a sweat or takes a hard hit in the open field. He knows all about the players and can rattle off their latest stats, but he doesn't know the players. He yells and cheers, but nothing is really required of him. There is no sacrifice he has to make. And the truth is, as excited as he seems, if the team he's cheering for starts to let him down and has a few off seasons, his passion will wane pretty quickly. After several losing seasons you can expect him to jump off the fan wagon and begin cheering for some other team. He is an enthusiastic admirer.

And I think Jesus has a lot of fans these days. Fans who cheer for him when things are going well, but who walk away when it's a difficult season. Fans who sit safely in the stands cheering, but they know nothing of the sacrifice and pain of the field. Fans who know all about Jesus, but they don't *know* him.

But Jesus was never interested in having fans. When he defines what kind of relationship he wants, "enthusiastic admirer" isn't an option. My concern is that many of our churches in America have gone from being sanctuaries to becoming stadiums. And every week all the fans come to the stadium where they cheer for Jesus but have no interest in truly following him. The biggest threat to the church today is fans who call themselves Christians but aren't actually interested in following Christ. They want to be close enough to Jesus to get all the benefits, but not so close that it requires anything from them.

So I invite you to find a seat in the back of a coffee shop and read on. Let's honestly and biblically define the relationship. Are you a follower of Jesus? Or are you really just a fan?

PART ONE
Fan or Follower?

ONE

A Decision or a Commitment?

John 3—Nicodemus

In John chapter 3 we read about a fan named Nicodemus. You should know that he wasn't just any fan. He was a well-known and well-respected man of God. Nicodemus was a member of the Sanhedrin, an elite group of community and religious leaders. He had been an admirer of Jesus for some time. Listening to the teaching of Jesus, he couldn't help but be inspired. He watched as Jesus worked incredible miracles, but it wasn't just his power that was impressive, it was also his compassion and love.

Nicodemus was ready to take his relationship

with Jesus to another level, but it wasn't that easy. It never is. There would be much to lose if he went public as a follower of Jesus. What would people think if they found out that Nicodemus was an admirer of this homeless carpenter-turned-rabbi from a nothing town called Nazareth? At the very least he would lose his position in the Sanhedrin and his reputation as a religious leader. Being a secret admirer of Jesus cost him nothing, but becoming a follower came with a high price tag. It always does.

So Nicodemus finds himself at what would seem to be a surprising crossroads: he has to choose between religion and a relationship with Jesus. There is no way for him to truly become a follower of Jesus without losing his religion. This wouldn't be the last time that religion would get in the way of someone following Jesus.

In John chapter 3 we read about his D.T.R. moment with Jesus. The story begins with the time of day it was when Nicodemus approached Jesus: "He came to Jesus at night . . ." (v. 2).

It would be easy to overlook this detail and dismiss it as insignificant. But ask yourself, *Why would he come to Jesus at night?* He had plenty of opportunities during the day. Jesus was teaching in public places where it would have been quite convenient for Nicodemus to talk to him for a few minutes. In fact, given his position as a religious leader, the other people would have quickly stepped out of the way for Nicodemus. But Scripture says, "He came to Jesus at night . . ."

At night no one would see him. At night he would avoid awkward questions from the other religious leaders. At night he could spend time with Jesus without anyone knowing. If he could speak with Jesus at night when no one was around, maybe he could begin a relationship with Jesus without having to make any real changes. He could follow Jesus without it impacting his job. In fact, his friends and family wouldn't even have to know. He could talk to Jesus at night and quietly make a decision in his heart to believe in Jesus; that way it wouldn't disrupt his comfortable and established life. That sounds like a lot of fans I know. Fans are happy to follow Jesus as long as that doesn't require any significant changes or have negative implications.

Here is the reality that Nicodemus is about to have impressed upon him: There is no way to follow Jesus without him interfering with your life. Following Jesus will cost you something. Following Jesus always costs something. For Nicodemus, following Jesus would cost him a powerful position. It would cost him the respect of his coworkers. It would cost him his source of income and livelihood.

It would cost him friendships. It would likely cost him some family relationships. This brings up a very telling question for most fans: Has following Jesus cost you anything? I don't mean for that to be a rhetorical question. Take a moment and jot down what following Jesus has cost you. How has following Jesus interfered with your life?

Most of us don't mind Jesus making some minor change in our lives, but Jesus wants to turn our lives upside down. Fans don't mind him doing a little touch-up work, but Jesus wants complete renovation. Fans come to Jesus thinking tune-up, but Jesus is thinking overhaul. Fans want Jesus to inspire them, but Jesus wants to interfere with their lives.

Nicodemus begins his conversation with Jesus by making it clear that he has decided that Jesus really is from God. He had come to a point of belief, but where would he go from there? Jesus doesn't waste time. He tells Nicodemus in verse 3 that he must be born again. That would have been hard for this religious leader to hear. He had memorized the first five books of the Bible when he was a boy and had spent his adult life building a religious resume. But Jesus makes it clear to Nicodemus that those righteous acts and religious rituals are not the measurements he is using. Nicodemus must humble himself and be born again into a whole new way of life.

Nicodemus had made a decision about Jesus, but that's not the same as following him. Jesus would not accept a relationship with Nicodemus where he simply believed; Jesus wanted Nicodemus to follow. Jesus didn't just want Nicodemus at night; he wanted Nicodemus during the day too.

Diagnosing Fandom—Question 1: Have You Made a Decision for Jesus, or Have You Committed to Jesus?

There is a difference. There shouldn't be. But there is a difference. Many have made a decision to believe in Jesus without making a commitment to follow Jesus. The gospel allows for no such distinction. Biblical belief is more than mental assent or verbal acknowledgment. Many fans have repeated a prayer or raised their hand or walked forward at the end of a sermon and made a decision to believe, but there was never a commitment to follow. Jesus never offered such an option. He is looking for more than words of belief; he's looking to see how those words are lived out in your life. When we decide to believe in Jesus without making a commitment to follow him, we become nothing more than fans.

We tend to define belief as the acceptance of

something as real or true. But biblical belief is more than just an intellectual acceptance or a heartfelt acknowledgment; it is a commitment to follow. Following by definition requires more than mental assent; it calls for movement. One of the reasons our churches can become fan factories is that we often separate the two messages of "believe" and "follow."

If you read through the four Gospels that tell of Christ's life, you'll find that Jesus says "Believe in me" about five times. But care to guess how many times Jesus said "Follow me"? About twenty times. Now I'm not saying that following is more important than believing. What I am saying is that the two are firmly connected. They are the heart and lungs of faith. One can't live without the other. If you try and separate the message of follow from the message of believe, belief dies in the process. Our churches will continue to be full of fans until we break down the dichotomy between following and believing. Following is part of believing. To truly believe is to follow.

So in case someone left it out or forgot to mention it when they explained what it meant to be a Christian, let me be clear: There is no forgiveness without repentance. There is no salvation without surrender. There is no life without death. There is no believing without committing.

At the church where I am a pastor, someone

sent an email asking to be removed from the church membership. The stated reason for leaving read as follows:

I don't like Kyle's sermons.

That's all it said. That begs for some kind of explanation, so I decided to call the person. I checked the name of the person and got the phone number. I confirmed that it wasn't my wife. Then I called him on my cell phone. I would suggest that when making this type of call from your personal phone, first go to "Settings," then "Show my caller ID," and then turn to "Off." Do not attempt while driving.

When he answered I simply said, "Hey, this is Kyle Idleman. I understand you're leaving the church because you don't like my sermons."

There was a brief silence. I had caught him off guard, just as I'd planned. It was awkward for a moment, and then he started talking—rambling, really—trying to express what he meant. Somewhere in the middle of his lengthy explanation he said something. What he said was not meant to be encouraging, but his words caused me to breathe such a sigh of relief that tears came to my eyes. I wrote down what he said:

Well . . . whenever I listen to one of the messages, I feel like you are trying to interfere with my life.

Yeah, umm, that's kind of like my job description.

But do you hear what he was saying? He's saying, *I believe in Jesus, I'm a big fan, but don't ask me to follow. I don't mind coming to church on the weekends. I'll pray before meals. I'll even slap a Jesus fish on my bumper. But I don't want Jesus to interfere with my life.* When Jesus defines the relationship he wants with us, he makes it clear that being a fan who believes without making any real commitment to follow isn't an option.

When Nicodemus meets with Jesus in John 3 we're left wondering what he's going to do. The silence seemed to identify him as a fan who wasn't even an enthusiastic admirer, but a secret admirer who never managed the courage to take his relationship with Jesus from words of belief to a life of commitment.

But it turns out this isn't the last we read of Nicodemus. The next time we meet up with him is in John 7. The popularity of Jesus has grown immensely. The religious leaders are overcome with jealousy and fear. We read that the Sanhedrin meet together to find a reason to silence Jesus. Part of their role as religious leaders is to judge false prophets. They need to drum up some kind of accusation or charge that will indict Jesus as a false teacher. Nicodemus is sitting among his peers as they conspire to bring Jesus down. He is just one of the seventy-two religious leaders in this ruling body. Nicodemus believes Jesus is from God, but his mind is racing with what it's going to cost him if he goes public with his conviction. Then we read in verse 51 that Nicodemus comes to the defense of Jesus:

> "Does our law condemn a man without first hearing him to find out what he has been doing?"

Though he stops short of saying what he believes, he does risk his career and reputation and publicly speaks up on behalf of Jesus. This is no longer a private conversation about what he believes. He allows what he believes to interfere with his work, his relationships, and his financial future. In that moment he stops being just a fan and begins the journey of following.

When he speaks out in defense of Jesus, we read in verse 52 that the rest of the Sanhedrin respond this way:

> "Are you from Galilee, too?"

I know that doesn't seem very harsh, but they are clearly trying to embarrass Nicodemus for associating with Jesus. Nazareth was a small, insignificant town that no one was proud to be from. Apparently they even had a saying in those days, "Can anything good come out of Nazareth?" The Sanhedrin laughed at Jesus because of where he was from, and now they used it to attack Nicodemus. It was meant to be a hard shot to his ego and a threat to the religious reputation that he had worked so hard to establish. It was a reality check for Nicodemus.

I've discovered there is almost always a moment like this for believers. They are put in a position where they have to decide between being a fan or a follower.

Any hope Nicodemus had that he could follow Jesus without it interfering with his life was shot down with that one question, *"Are you from Galilee, too?"*

At the end of John's gospel, there is one other brief reference to Nicodemus. In John chapter 19 Jesus has been crucified and his body is being prepared for burial. And then we read that Nicodemus brings "a mixture of myrrh and aloes, about seventy-five pounds" (v. 39). This is an extremely expensive and costly gesture. And make no mistake, this gesture costs him more than just money. There is no longer any chance of hiding his affection.

In fact, when most others have abandoned Jesus, or are hiding in fear, Nicodemus makes this great gesture of affection and devotion. Things have moved past words of belief expressed in the darkness of night. He's no longer a secret admirer. He's not just an enthusiastic admirer. It seems he has become a follower. That's the last time we read of Nicodemus in Scripture. Christian tradition asserts that he was martyred sometime in the first century.

If you have believed in darkness, Jesus now invites you to follow him in the light.

TWO

Knowledge about Him or Intimacy with Him?

Luke 7

In the Bible, we read about a group of religious leaders known as the Pharisees. The Pharisees knew a lot about God. When someone wanted to play "Bible Trivial Pursuit," they would dominate. They knew about God, but what we discover is they really didn't *know* him.

In Matthew 15:8 Jesus describes the Pharisees this way:

> "These people honor me with their lips, but their hearts are far from me."

That description seems to fit most fans I know. Like the Pharisees, many fans give their minds to the study of God, but they never surrender their hearts. These were men who had plenty of knowledge about God, but they didn't really know God. This is what often separates the fans from the followers. It's the difference between knowledge and intimacy.

In Luke 7, Jesus has been invited over for dinner by one of these Pharisees. His name was Simon. Most likely Simon extended the invitation after Jesus finished teaching. Apparently, this was before the days of having a potluck meal after the sermon. For Simon, having the visiting rabbi over for a meal would have been considered a religious merit. Jesus should have been considered the guest of honor for this meal, but it quickly becomes apparent that Simon was spending time with Jesus out of a sense of duty instead of a desire to honor him.

There were certain rules of etiquette at a dinner like this. For instance, the customary greeting for an honored guest would have been a kiss. If the guest was a person of equal social rank, then the host would greet the guest with a kiss on the cheek. If it was a person of especially high honor, the host would greet the guest with a kiss on the hand. Neglecting the kiss of greeting was equivalent to openly ignoring somebody. It would be like having a person come into your home and refusing to even acknowledge their presence in some way. Not saying hi, not shaking their hand, not even giving them the head nod while simultaneously raising the eyebrows, nothing.

Another part of first-century Middle Eastern etiquette involved the washing of feet. The washing of feet was mandatory before meals. If you truly wanted to honor the guest, then you would do it yourself. If not, you might have your servant wash the feet of your honored guest. At the very least you would simply give the water to your guest to wash his or her own feet.

For an especially distinguished guest, you might also give them some olive oil for anointing their head. This was inexpensive oil, but it was still considered an especially hospitable gesture. But when Jesus came to the house of Simon, there was no kiss of greeting. There was no washing of feet. There was no oil for his head. And these were not accidental oversights. This was quite deliberate. Jesus was ignored and insulted.

Don't miss the irony of this moment. Simon had spent his life studying the Scriptures. By the time he was twelve he had the first twelve books of the Bible memorized. By the time he was fifteen he had memorized the entire Old Testament. He had committed to memory the more than three hundred prophecies about the coming Messiah. Yet he didn't realize it was the Messiah who now sat at his table with a hand that hadn't been kissed, feet that hadn't been washed, and a head that hadn't been anointed. He knew all about Jesus, but he didn't know Jesus.

Diagnosing Fandom—Question 2: Do You Just Know about Jesus, or Do You Really Know Him?

Fans have a tendency to confuse their knowledge for intimacy. They don't recognize the difference between knowing about Jesus and truly knowing Jesus. In church we've often got this confused. We have established systems of learning that result in knowledge, but not necessarily intimacy.

Now don't get me wrong, studying and learning from God's Word is invaluable. Jesus referenced, read, and quoted all kinds of passages from the Old Testament, ample proof that he had studied God's Word with great care and diligence. The problem isn't knowledge. The problem is that you can have knowledge without having intimacy. In fact, knowledge can be a false indicator of intimacy. Clearly where there is intimacy there should be a growing knowledge, but too often there is knowledge without a growing intimacy. Part of the proof that I have an intimate relationship with my wife is how much I know about her. I know what kind of shampoo she uses. I know what kind of sushi she orders. I know what makes her laugh and what makes her cry. So knowledge is part of intimacy, but just because there is knowledge doesn't mean there is intimacy.

Yada, Yada, Yada

Probably the best biblical word for intimacy is the word *know*. But this knowing goes much deeper than knowledge. The Bible first uses this word to describe a relationship in Genesis 4:1:

> Adam *knew* Eve his wife (NKJV, emphasis added).

The Hebrew word for *knew* here is the word *yada'*. Here's the best way to define the word *yada'*: *to know completely and to be completely known.*

But the NIV translates the word a little differently, because it puts it in context of what's happening. So your Bible probably says in Genesis 4:1:

> Adam made love to his wife Eve . . .

You get the picture? That is our context for *yada'*. Now don't just giggle and brush past this. This is not just a "yada, yada, yada" moment, okay? This is a *YADA'* moment between a husband and a wife. It's this intimate connection on every level. To know and to be known completely. It's a beautiful picture that helps us get at what it really means to know Christ. There are other Hebrew words that could have been used to describe the sexual intimacy that is taking place. These words for sex are used later in Scripture and refer to the physical act or even procreation. But the word in Genesis 4 is *yada'*, the Hebrew word for "know." Clearly when the Bible uses this word for "know" it means much more than knowledge. It describes the most intimate of connections. One Hebrew scholar defines the word this way: "A mingling of the souls." That's more than knowledge—that's intimacy.

So now you understand that this word translated "know" is used to describe a man and a woman being intimate with one another. They *yada'* each other. With that in mind I want to talk to you about how God wants to know and be known by us. What I'm about to tell you will seem a little bit strange to some of you, a little bit weird. I get that. We can work through some of the weirdness, but I at least wanted to give you a heads-up going into it.

If you trace the usage of *yada'* through the Old Testament, you'll find that over and over again, this is the same word that's used to describe God's relationship with us. The same word used to describe the connection between a man and a wife is used to describe how God knows you and how he wants to be known by you. This completely changed the way I defined my relationship with Jesus. I began to see what he wanted from me as a follower. Instead of identifying myself as a follower because I know *about* Jesus, I understand that I am a follower because I *know* Jesus.

In Luke 7, the Pharisee knew all about Jesus, but he didn't know Jesus. His heart was far from him. He didn't know that the visiting rabbi sitting at his table was the promised Messiah that he had spent countless hours studying about.

Luke tells us that while Jesus is eating at this Pharisee's house a woman comes on the scene. They were likely eating in a courtyard area where people could watch and even listen in on the conversation. But things start to get awkward when this woman comes uninvited up to the table where they are eating. To better comprehend the tension of this moment, understand that this wasn't just any woman. Verse 37 tells us that she "lived a sinful life." More specifically, she was a known prostitute in the village.

Apparently she had heard Jesus teaching, maybe earlier in the day, and something happened in her heart.

She was desperate to see Jesus again, and she overheard someone saying that he was having dinner at the home of Simon the Pharisee—a dinner she would never be invited to attend, not in a thousand years. Of course, normally she would have no interest in attending. She had felt the condemning glares of the Pharisees enough to stay as far away as possible from places like Simon's house. But she had to see Jesus. It's hard to imagine what it would take for her to walk into that courtyard. But she is so focused on Jesus that she forgets about herself. She is desperate to express the love and affection she feels for him. What she does next is reckless, it's impulsive, it's inappropriate, and it's exactly the kind of follower Jesus wants.

Picture the scene. Jesus is reclining at the table. Instead of using chairs they would lean on an elbow that was propped up by a cushion. Their feet would be away from the table. This woman approaches and stands at the filthy feet of Jesus. The table grows silent. Everybody is watching. Everybody knows who she is. *What is she doing?* She looks around at the guests. She feels from some that familiar glare of condemnation. Others keep their eyes down, embarrassed by her presence and the awkwardness of the moment. But when she looks at Jesus, he seems to know what has happened in her heart. He gives her a warm smile. He seems delighted that she has come, and he looks at her with the eyes of a loving father watching his beautiful daughter as she enters the room. She has never had a man look at her that way before. She is so undone by this that the tears come, just a few at first, and then more. She falls to the ground and begins to kiss his feet. Soon, the tears are just pouring down her face. They begin to drip onto the dirty feet of Jesus. As she looks at the muddy streaks she suddenly realizes that his feet haven't been washed. She can't ask for a towel, so she lets down her hair. In those days women always wore their hair up in public. For a woman to wear her hair down in front of a man that was not her husband was considered to be such an intimate expression that it was literally grounds for divorce. She lets her hair down in front of Jesus and begins washing Jesus' feet with her tears and drying them with her hair.

Then Luke says she had an alabaster jar of ointment. Most likely this refers to a flask that was often worn around the neck as a kind of perfume for women. As you might guess, because of her profession, this flask was quite important. She had used it a drop at a time many, many times, for many men. But now she empties it. She just empties the whole thing out. She will not need it anymore. She pours this flask, her life, on his feet, and she kisses them over and over. At the end of the story Jesus says to Simon:

> "Look at this woman kneeling here. When I entered your home, you didn't offer me water to wash the dust from my feet, but she has washed them with her tears and wiped them with her hair. You didn't greet me with a kiss, but from the time I first came in, she has not stopped kissing my feet. You neglected the courtesy of olive oil to anoint my head, but she has anointed my feet with rare perfume."
>
> Luke 7:44–46 NLT

In the end, the religious leader with all the knowledge is the fan, and the prostitute who intimately expressed her love for Jesus is shown to be the follower. Here, then, is the question you and I have to ask ourselves:

Who am I most like in the story?

When is the last time you had a moment with Jesus like this woman in Luke 7 had? When's the last time you've poured yourself out before him? When is the last time the tears streamed down your face as you expressed your love for him? When is the last time you demonstrated your love for him with reckless abandonment?

I am not asking if you know about him; I am asking if you know him.

THREE

One of Many or Your One and Only?

Luke 14

In the fourteenth chapter of Luke's gospel Jesus has another D.T.R. talk, but this time it isn't one-on-one in the shadows of the night or sitting around a dinner table. This time Jesus speaks to an entire crowd. By this point in Jesus' life, word had spread about this incredible teacher who made the lame walk, the blind see, and who turned funeral processions into family reunions. People were coming from all over and filling the hillsides. I imagine the scenes really did have the atmosphere of a stadium full of raving fans.

For a while Jesus seemed okay with the large crowds. He was fine with people coming out to be inspired by his teaching. He didn't seem to mind the fact that they were coming to see some miracles. No doubt many of them showed up carrying popcorn with extra butter, ready for the entertainment to begin. Jesus welcomed people who were curious and wanting to find out more about this unconventional rabbi.

But the time comes when he wants to talk about the relationship. He draws a line in the sand and wants to know where these people stand. Ultimately what concerns Jesus the most isn't the size of the crowd, it's the level of commitment.

Have they just come for a miracle and healing show? Do they just want to hear a motivational speaker? We're about to find out because this crowd is going to be separated into two groups: fans and followers.

> Large crowds were traveling with Jesus, and turning to them he said: "If anyone comes to me and does not hate father and mother, wife and children, brothers and sisters—yes, even their own life—such a person cannot be my disciple."
>
> Luke 14:25–26

That doesn't seem very seeker-sensitive at all. You would think it would read:

> *A large crowd was following Jesus. He turned around and said to them, "What a great crowd! I want everyone to go invite one friend and come back tonight for a carnival. We'll have live music. All the loaves and fish you can eat. We'll even have a water-to-wine booth. And whoever invites the most friends gets one free miracle. Let's pack this hillside out!"*

Instead he tells the people that if they want to follow him, they must hate their family, even their own lives.

What the what?

Where did that come from? I'm sure that about this time, some of the fans began to pack up and head home. It was fun while it lasted, but this isn't what they signed up for.

So the big question is, *Does following Jesus really mean that you have to hate your grandma?*

Obviously hating your family would contradict the other teachings of Jesus. So why the strong language? Maybe Jesus uses such dramatic language here because in this culture if you were to become a follower of Jesus without your family's blessing, you would have been thought of as hating your family. A decision to follow Jesus would have been interpreted as turning your back on your family and walking away from them.

Jesus is honest with the crowd about what it may cost to follow him. He lets them know that following him may mean offending your parents or grandparents. It may mean being cut out of the will or even cut off from the family. I've talked to people who put off following Jesus because they don't want to hurt their parents' feelings. I have had more than one person tell me that when their grandma dies they plan on becoming a Christian. They decide to wait because they don't want to upset her.

And maybe as you sit in the crowd it seems that Jesus is talking directly to you. You know that your dad won't approve. He'll roll his eyes and mumble something about you getting carried away. Your brother or sister won't know what to make of your decision to follow, and they may distance themselves from you. Your boyfriend or girlfriend may very well break up with you. You can hear your friends laughing behind your back about you finding religion. There's a good chance your husband will make fun of you or your wife will criticize you. And Jesus is saying, "Yep, that may be part of it. And if you're not willing to choose me over your family, then you are not ready to follow, and maybe it's time for you to go on home."

The word *hate* is defined as "to dislike something intensely" or to have "feelings of intense hostility." Clearly Jesus doesn't want us to hate our family in that sense. It would violate everything else the Bible teaches on the subject. Jesus himself said one of the two greatest commandments was, "Love your neighbor as yourself." Our families are the closest neighbors we have. Here's how the New Living Translation version of the Bible puts it:

> "If you want to be my disciple, you must, by comparison, hate everyone else—your father and mother, wife and children, brothers and sisters . . ."
>
> LUKE 14:26 NLT

The NLT says "hate." The Contemporary English Version says "love me more." The most accurate understanding of what Jesus is requiring of his followers is a combination of these two translations. Jesus is most likely conveying the idea of "love me more," but "hate" is also accurate, because it captures the degree to which we love Jesus more. Imagine that the different loves of your life are competing in a race to see who wins first place. Jesus, your spouse, your children, a best friend, and a sibling are all lined up on the starting blocks. The idea isn't that Jesus comes in first place in this race. What Jesus is describing here is more accurately understood by picturing a race for first place in your life where he is the only one on the track. Jesus isn't just saying, "I want to be first place in your life." He is saying, "I don't even want there to be a second place." When we compare our relationship with him to anyone else, there should be no competition. Fans will try and make Jesus one of many. Some fans may even make Jesus the first of many. But when Jesus defines the relationship he makes it clear; he wants to be your one and only.

Diagnosing Fandom—Question 3: Is Jesus One of Many, or Is He Your One and Only?

Let me take you back to a D.T.R. talk you've had at some point with someone special. If you're married, it's probably best to picture your husband or wife. Now imagine that while you are defining the relationship and determining the level of commitment, you make it clear where you stand. You are all-in. You say, "*I am giving you my heart and want nothing more than to spend the rest of my life with you.*" Now imagine that your significant other says something like this to you: "*I love you too. I am willing to commit to you for the rest of my life. Let's take this to the next level. I just have one condition; I still want to be able to see other people.*"

That is essentially what a fan says to Jesus. A fan says, "*I love you. I am committed to you. But let's not be exclusive.*" Or imagine that after you have the D.T.R. talk you carry your girlfriend's picture in your wallet. As soon as it's opened her picture is the first thing you see. When she opens your wallet and sees her picture she thinks it's sweet, but imagine that behind her picture are pictures of the last three or four girls you have dated. That's going to be a problem. It's not enough for her to be first; she will insist on being "the only." Jesus makes it clear that he will not share your affection. Following him requires your whole heart.

I want to ask you some questions to help reveal if Jesus is one of many, or your one and only. These are not rhetorical questions. Take time to think about your answers. How you answer these questions can help show you what is competing with Jesus for your affection.

1. **For what do you sacrifice your money?** The Bible says, "where your treasure is, there your heart will be also" (Matt. 6:21). What you spend your time and money on often reveals the true desire of your heart and shows who or what you are truly following. The reason Jesus talked more about money than any other subject is because it can easily become his chief competition. We end up following money and the things money can buy instead of Jesus.
2. **When you're hurt, where do you go for comfort?** When you experience the pain of this life where do you turn? Maybe it's to a parent or a spouse. Maybe it's to the refrigerator. Isn't that why they call it comfort food? Do you bury yourself in work? All these things have the potential to compete with Jesus for our devotion and affection. There is certainly nothing wrong with finding comfort from family and friends; that's part of God's design. But the question is: Do they take the place of Jesus?
3. **What disappoints or frustrates you the most?** When we feel overwhelmed with disappointment, it often reveals that something has become too important. It may be

something as significant as a loss of a job or something as insignificant as the loss of a ball game. When we find that those things have the power to determine who we are and what kind of day we have, it very well may be evidence that something is more important than it should be. Of course some level of disappointment and frustration can be natural. But if you find that you are excessively disappointed or overly frustrated, it's an indication of what might be competing for affection that is to be Christ's alone.

4. **What is it that really gets you excited?** Recently I was watching a college football game on TV when my twelve-year-old daughter came in and said, "I've never seen you so excited." She had seen me baptize new believers. She saw my reaction to the birth of her baby brother. She had seen me take her out for many daddy-daughter dates. But she had never seen me more excited than watching a college football game. *Ouch.*

   Like the things that disappoint us, the things that excite us can also point to something or someone that is in competition with Jesus. Could it be sports, decorating, music, work, or your appearance? All these things are fine and good, but they have the potential to become a type of mistress that is robbing God of your whole heart.

John Oros was a church leader in Romania during the communist era. When he spoke at the Associated Mennonite Biblical Seminary, he talked about what that was like:

During communism, many of us preached . . . and people came at the end of a service, and they said, "I have decided to become a Christian." We told them, "It is good that you want to become a Christian, but we would like to tell you that there is a price to be paid. Why don't you reconsider what you want to do, because many things can happen to you. You can lose, and you can lose big."

John said that a high percentage of them chose to take part in a three-month class to better understand the decision they were making. John says:

At the end of this period, many participants declared their desire to be baptized. Typically, I would respond, "It's really nice that you want to become a Christian, but when you give your

> *testimony, there will be informers here who will jot down your name. Tomorrow the problems will start. Count the cost. Christianity is not easy. It's not cheap. You can be demoted. You can lose your job. You can lose your friends. You can lose your neighbors. You can lose your kids. You can lose even your own life."*

He wanted the people to get to a place where following Jesus was so important to them, that if they lost everything it would still be worth it.

If following Jesus cost you everything, would it still be worth it?

FOUR

Following Jesus or Following the Rules?

Matthew 23

In Matthew 23, Jesus tries to get the attention of a group of fans known as the religious leaders. If you were trying to determine who were the fans and who were the followers in Jesus' day, these religious leaders would likely be identified as the followers. They had a mastery of the Scriptures and were considered expert theologians. They were especially known for their strict observance of the law. They would have received high scores for their religious rule keeping, but that's not what Jesus was most concerned about. Following the rules kept them focused on the outside, but who they were on the inside was what Jesus paid attention to. And the problem with these religious leaders was that, like many fans, who they were on the outside didn't match up with what was on the inside.

In this chapter Jesus preaches one of his last sermons here on earth, and it's directed right at these religious leaders. He doesn't hold anything back. If you grew up thinking of Jesus as a Mr. Rogers of Nazareth who was always smiling, winking at people, and wearing a sweater-vest, the tone Jesus takes with these religious leaders may surprise you. The name of the sermon we're going to study is not "Won't You Be My Neighbor?" This sermon is traditionally called "The Seven Woes."

The word *woe* is an onomatopoeia—a word where the definition comes from its sound. The word *woe* is both an expression of grief and a curse. Seven times in his sermon Jesus says, "Woe to you . . ." Each "woe" is followed by a scathing rebuke. He isn't cautioning the religious leaders. He isn't offering them counsel or advice. Jesus is going to strongly oppose these religious leaders because he doesn't want people to confuse following the rules with following him. His indictments against these religious leaders should serve as a warning to those fans who consider themselves followers because of their religious rule-keeping and Christian credentials.

The Fan Club

These spiritual leaders Jesus is addressing in Matthew 23 made up a religious ruling body of seventy-two men called the Sanhedrin. Within the Sanhedrin there were two different groups called the Sadducees and the Pharisees. These two groups did not get along. When interpreting Scripture the Sadducees were very liberal, and the Pharisees were quite conservative. The Sadducees served the roles of Chief Priests and Elders. If you were a Sadducee, it meant you were born into that position. There were, of course, other requirements, but it had to be part of your heritage. But being a part of the Pharisees didn't depend on the family you were born into; it depended on your hard work. Becoming a Pharisee required an incredible amount of textual study and theological training. And what I've noticed is that many fans fit into one of these two camps.

Some fans are like the Sadducees. Their faith was something they were born into. It was never really something they chose. Maybe when you were born your parents handed you a mask, and you grew up acting like Christians act, talking how Christians talked, listening to the music Christians listened to, but you never fell in love with Jesus. Your faith has always been more about honoring your heritage than surrendering your heart.

On the other hand, some fans are like the Pharisees. They would measure their faith by their hard work at learning and following the law.

Diagnosing Fandom—Question 4: Are You More Focused on the Outside Than the Inside?

The main problem Jesus had with these religious leaders is they were hypocrites. I'm not guessing at that; that's what he calls them. To their faces. Eight times. The word *hypocrite* comes from Greek ancient classical theater. Greek actors were called *hypocrites*. Often, a single actor would play several different characters, and for each character, the actor would use a different mask. So when they would switch characters, they would switch masks. Imagine a television show like *The Brady Bunch* done in Greek theater. One person might play all the different parts. The actor uses one mask when playing Jan, and another mask when playing Marcia. Each character uses a different mask, but you never really see the actor's face. The actor is always behind one of these masks. And fans get caught up on what people see on the outside, but it's just a mask. What other people see doesn't reflect who they really are. Jesus says in verse 5:

> "Everything they do is for show" (NLT).

As a recovering hypocrite, I can tell you that some fans can be almost impossible to identify because they deliver Oscar-worthy performances as they play the role of a follower. When Jesus begins his sermon in Matthew 23 he is speaking to the people about the religious leaders while they listen in:

> Then Jesus said to the crowds and to His disciples: "The teachers of the law and the Pharisees sit in Moses' seat. So you must be careful to do everything they tell you" (vv. 1–3a).

I wonder if Jesus paused here for a moment. The Pharisees think, *Okay, this is more like it. He's finally coming over to our side. He's pointing to us as the authorities.* But Jesus continues:

> "But do not do what they do, for they do not practice what they preach" (v. 3b).

The problem that Jesus has with these teachers is that what they are teaching isn't a reflection of who they really are.

These religious types are the fans that Jesus seems to have the most trouble with. Fans who will walk into a restaurant and bow their heads to pray before a meal just in case someone is watching. Fans who won't go to R-rated movies at the theater but have a number of them saved on their DVR at home. Fans who may feed the hungry and help the needy, and then they make sure they work it into every conversation for the next two weeks. Fans who make sure people see them put in their offering at church, but they haven't considered reaching out to their neighbor who lost a job and can't pay the bills. Fans who like seeing other people fail because in their minds it makes them look better. Fans whose primary concern in raising their children is what other people think. Fans who are reading this and assuming I'm describing someone else. Fans who have worn the mask for so long they have fooled even themselves.

Jesus has harsh words for these fans who try to impress others through their religious credentials. It's interesting to note that as severe as Jesus is with these religious leaders, he is just as tender and encouraging to those who have genuinely given him their hearts, even if they don't have it all together on the outside.

Please don't miss this: Jesus doesn't expect followers to be perfect, but he does call them to be authentic.

Every week I get a chance to sit down with the people who are new to our church. On any given week there are anywhere from two to twenty people sitting around a table. They have a chance to tell their story, and I have an opportunity to listen and pray for them. Typically we have two separate kinds of people in that room. There are some who have been around the church and God for a good part of their lives. They know the rules. They know what to say and how to say it. They know what words to include and what parts of their stories to leave out. They've learned to wear a mask.

Then there are those who are new to Christ and the church. They haven't learned the rules. And when they tell their story they will include a marriage that fell apart because of their unfaithfulness. They just don't know any better. It's not uncommon for their stories to begin "I've been sober for . . ." and sometimes it's been years. Sometimes it's been days. I've heard ex-cons talk about their crimes. I've heard men talk about pornography and women talk about credit card debt. Parents will talk about how much they are struggling with their kids. Many times a couple will say that their marriage is just barely hanging on. They'll tell about eating disorders, gambling problems, and drug addictions. They just don't know any better. And I hope nobody tells them that they're supposed to act like they've got it all together. You don't often get to see people without a mask. And it's such a beautiful thing.

Jesus speaks so strongly to these rule-loving religious leaders because he knows that when following him becomes about following the rules, people end up walking away from both.

I grew up going to a Christian school. It was a great school, but there were a lot of rules. You couldn't have your hair over your ears if you were a boy. Girls' skirts couldn't be more than a couple of inches above their knees. Boys had to wear collared shirts. Girls had certain rules about makeup and jewelry. Now don't misunderstand what I'm saying, I don't think any of these rules were wrong or inappropriate. I think it's fine and good for a school or parents to establish such rules or guidelines. But here's what happened—a lot of my friends didn't associate all of those rules and regulations with school. Instead they connected the rules and regulations with being a Christian. For years they identified themselves as Christians and pointed to things like their short hair and collared shirts as evidence. When they got older they didn't like the rules, and because they associated following a bunch of rules with following Jesus, they walked away from both.

When we learn to truly follow Jesus, we find that obedience to God comes from the inside out. Submission to what God wants for our lives flows naturally out of that relationship. It's not to say that what we do or don't do doesn't matter, but what we do or don't do must come from who we are as followers of Jesus.

Maybe you grew up in a home where you were taught all about Jesus. Through fear and guilt you learned to keep as many of the rules as possible, hoping it would be enough to keep you out of hell. You were taught to observe different religious traditions and rituals in an effort to appease God. Instead of becoming a follower of Christ, you became a follower of religion.

It's not unusual for me to talk to Christian parents who are concerned because their college-age kids or grown children don't go to church and show almost no interest in Jesus or anything spiritual for that matter. Often these good churchgoing folks don't understand where things went wrong. They want to know what happened and what to do now. Well, there are no easy answers. Usually I listen to their story and offer a little encouragement and I pray with them.

A few months ago I was speaking in Houston, Texas, and a good-sized man, with a good-sized belt buckle, came up to me with tears in his eyes. He began to tell me the story of his prodigal daughter, how she went to college and totally turned her back on the faith. As soon as he started the story I knew how it would go. I've heard it so many times, even the details seem predictable. But when he finished, he didn't ask me why she was doing this or what had gone wrong. He wasn't looking for an explanation. Instead, with one sentence he put his finger on what he thought happened. Here's what he said . . .

> *We raised her in Church, but we didn't raise her in Christ.*

You hear what he is saying? We raised her to look right on the outside but didn't teach her about the inside. We taught her to keep all the rules, but she never really had a relationship. We made her feel guilty for the wrong things she did, but somehow she missed God's amazing grace.

We taught her to be a fan of Jesus—instead of a follower of Jesus.

FIVE

Self-Empowered or Spirit-Filled?

John 16

For some who are fans, I know just the title of this chapter makes them a little nervous. When you read "Spirit-filled," you got a little bit uncomfortable. Fans tend to be comfortable talking about God and Jesus, but the third member is kind of like the Cousin Eddie of the Trinity; you just don't know what to do with him. It reminds me of how I'm treated by my in-laws. I married a girl from a small Kansas town. She grew up on a farm several miles down a dirt road. In high school she raised pigs and drove a tractor. Her family tries to make me feel welcome, but whenever I show up I can almost hear that old *Sesame Street* song in the background, *One of these things is not like the other. One of these things just doesn't belong.*

The rest of the men show up for Thanksgiving wearing camo sprayed with deer urine, ready to go hunting after the big meal. I sit at the table in my designer shirt that is referred to as a "blouse" behind my back. I eat in silence as the men take turns telling about the deer they shot and the buck that got away. About a half hour after lunch, I look around and realize that I'm the only grown man in the house. I walk into the kitchen, where the ladies are making pies, and ask, "Do you know where the men went?" My mother-in-law says, and I quote, "All the men are outside." Hello? Um . . . clearly they're not *all* outside.

Now, I know they believe in my existence. I would even say that most of them like me. But they aren't sure what to do with me. I think that's how fans tend to approach the Holy Spirit. But the truth is, you cannot be a follower unless you are filled with the Holy Spirit.

Fans who try to follow Jesus without this power will start to show signs. Sooner or later they will reach a point where they are frustrated by failures. You keep doing what you don't want to do, and you don't do the things you really want to do. You promise others that you will change. "Things are going to be different this time," you say. And this time you really mean it. But the change rarely lasts more than a few days. You lie awake at night and promise yourself "Never again" . . . *never again will I lose my temper . . . never again will I get on that website . . . never again will I take a drink . . . never again.* But soon you're lying awake making the same promises. It just doesn't work. When we try to follow Jesus without being filled daily with the Spirit, we find ourselves frustrated by our failures and exhausted by our efforts.

Recently my wife and I and our four kids flew into the Atlanta airport from the island of Hispaniola where we had spent a month on a mission trip. After landing, we grabbed our bags and began a long hike through the airport. When we travel, my wife and I share the responsibilities. One of us packs lots of stuff, and one of us carries it everywhere. That's how we've worked it out.

So there I am, carrying about a half dozen bags through the airport. They are hanging all around me. It's just a moving pile of bags with my head sticking out of the top. We turn to go down a hallway that is about 100 yards long. My wife and kids all get on a moving sidewalk, but I'm carrying a wide load and it's impossible for me to navigate the turn and I miss the on-ramp.

They set the few bags they have on the moving sidewalk and just stand there watching me. I'm sweating like . . . well, like a man carrying a half dozen suitcases through the airport. I'm trying to keep up with the pace. We end up arriving at the end of the sidewalk at about the same time. But there's a difference. I'm frustrated, exhausted, and annoyed, and they are ready to keep moving. That's what our lives look like when we try the self-empowered hike, instead of the Spirit-filled walkway. Fans try to play the role of the Holy Spirit, but trying to be God has a tendency to wear you out. It will leave you tired and frustrated.

Fans trying to follow without being filled with the power of the Holy Spirit become overwhelmed by life's circumstances. They seem to be following Christ, but then something in life goes wrong and they don't have the power to overcome it. Instead of following Christ and sticking close to him in the storm, they become discouraged and keep their distance.

Eventually something happens, and you can't get through it on your own. Followers have discovered that it doesn't work without the power of the Spirit.

Diagnosing Fandom—Question 5: Are You a Self-Empowered Fan or a Spirit-Filled Follower?

In John 16 we read one of the last conversations Jesus has with his disciples before his arrest and crucifixion. He's trying to prepare them for his death, but they are in denial. They can't imagine losing Jesus as their leader, teacher, and friend. It's the worst possible news. But here's what Jesus says to them:

> "But very truly I tell you, it is for your good that I am going away. Unless I go away, the Advocate will not come to you; but if I go, I will send him to you."
>
> John 16:7

Did you catch that? Jesus, God in the flesh, says it's better for him to leave, because when he goes the Holy Spirit will come. It's better. Why would he say that? When I was in seminary I did a study of the references in the Bible that speak of God being *with* man. The Bible speaks of God being *with* Abraham. God was *with* Joseph. God was *with* Elisha. I noticed that most all of the references of "God being *with*" were in the Old Testament. They just weren't in the New Testament. I couldn't figure out why that was. I kept thinking I was missing something. Here's what I discovered: there is a subtle but critical prepositional change from the Old Testament to the New Testament. In the Old Testament it says "God *with* us"—but in the New Testament it's "God *in* us." Jesus says, "It's better for you if I go"—because while God with you is good, God in you is better. Jesus could be *with* his followers, but the Holy Spirit would live *in* his followers.

Sometimes I hear people talk about the different men and women of the Old Testament, and there is a hint of jealousy. They may say it, or just insinuate it, but here's what they communicate . . .

"What would it have been like to hear God's voice and see him move in such powerful ways? I wish it was the same for us as it was for those whose stories we read about in Scripture. When I get to heaven I can't wait to ask David, Elijah, or Moses what it was like."

But I think it will be just the opposite in heaven. Before we can ask David what it was like to slay the giant, to win the battles, he'll say, *"Tell me what it was like on earth to have the Holy Spirit living inside of you, giving you strength when you are weak."*

We might say to Elijah, *"What was it like to call down fire from heaven before the prophets of Baal and to raise that boy from the dead?"* And I think Elijah might say, *"Yeah, he actually ended up dying again. You tell me what it's like to have God living inside of you. What was it like to live life on earth with the Holy Spirit giving you joy when you're depressed or giving you the power to overcome that sin in your life?"*

We might say to Moses, *"What was it like to follow the cloud by day and the fire by night? What was it like to meet with God on that mountain?"* And Moses might say, *"I had to climb that mountain to meet with God. You tell me what it was like to have him dwell within you every day. What was it like to have the Holy Spirit giving you directions when you didn't know what to do or where to go?"*

In Romans 8:11 Paul illustrates just how powerful the Holy Spirit wants to be in our lives. He writes:

> The Spirit of God, who raised Jesus from the dead, lives in you (NLT).

The same Spirit that raised Christ from the dead now lives in his followers.

When you become a Christian, you receive from God the gift of the Holy Spirit. That's his promise to all who put their faith in him. So it's not a question of whether or not you have access to this power of the Holy Spirit; the question is, have you accessed it? Fans may have received the gift of the Holy Spirit, but they aren't being filled with the Holy Spirit.

This was a problem with the first-century church in Galatia. Paul had come in and preached a message of grace. People surrendered their lives to Christ and accepted his free gift. But soon after Paul headed out, a crew of false teachers known as the "Judaizers" came into the church and began pushing people back to the law. They began to put the emphasis on human effort and hard work rather than on the power of the Spirit. But here's how Paul addresses that:

> Are you so foolish? After beginning by means of the Spirit, are you now trying to finish by means of the flesh?
>
> GAL. 3:3

Paul points out that trying to live the Christian life out of your own power is ridiculous. Why would a person do that? Why would you walk when you can ride?

A surprising thing I've discovered over the years is that there are lots of churches like the one in Galatia. The message becomes "try harder," and the more people are around the church and the things of God, the more they slip into a "do-it-yourself" mentality. The emphasis is put more on their effort and self-discipline. Fans foolishly think that with enough hard work they can follow Jesus.

As ridiculous as it seems to put our confidence in our own efforts instead of the Holy Spirit's power, I can easily find myself trying to operate that way. This was especially true for me early on in ministry. Instead of admitting my weakness and declaring my complete dependence on God, I tried to do it myself.

When we moved from our last house into our current house, I saved the heaviest piece of furniture for last. It was the desk from my office. I tried to slide it, but the legs kept getting caught. Eventually I figured out that if I flipped it over so the top was on the floor and the feet were up in the air I could slide it across the carpet. I was pushing with everything I had and was slowly making progress. About that time my four-year-old son came over and asked if he could help me. He stood between my arms and began to push. Together we started sliding it across the floor. He was pushing and grunting as we inched our way along. Then he stopped, looked up at me, and said, "Dad, you're in my way." I could push it just fine by myself. He couldn't budge it but insisted on doing it himself. He thought he was pushing the desk. I couldn't help but laugh.

When I started a new church in Los Angeles County, California, I found that I was overwhelmed with pressure and stress. I was working more than seventy hours a week. My wife would ask me to take a day off, and I would say, "I can't." When the church was about a year old, I woke up in the night and had this strange sense that God was laughing at me. I laid there trying to discern what it was about. Why was God laughing at me? I could never quite figure it out, but I often wondered what it meant. And then about five years later, when my son and I were pushing a desk across the floor and he looked up and said, "Dad, you're in my way," I understood. The moment I started laughing at my son's comment, that dream came back to my mind. And I realized why God was laughing at me. I thought I was pushing the desk. Instead of recognizing God's power and strength, I'd started to think it all depended on me.

Fans eventually get burned out from trying to live the Christian life out of their own efforts. If you are depending on your own strength to follow Christ, you will soon find yourself drained and defeated. Jesus promised his followers that the Spirit would come on them in power.

Followers of Jesus understand that it's a journey we are never to make alone. Instead we keep in step with the Spirit, and he supernaturally gives us the strength and the power we need.

SIX

The Relationship Defined

Matthew 7

Not long ago I was returning to Louisville from a quick trip to Cincinnati. There is a highway between Cincinnati and Louisville called I–71. It's a straight shot and takes about an hour. I was heading home in plenty of time to have dinner with my family. The radio was turned up, it was a beautiful day, and I was enjoying the journey. After about an hour I knew I was getting close to Louisville, but then I saw a sign that said, "Welcome to Lexington."

There is a place right outside Cincinnati where, if you're not careful, you can easily miss where I–71 towards Louisville splits off from I–75 towards Lexington. This is a frequent mistake and has happened to a lot of people making this trip. For close to an hour I was completely convinced I was on I–71, but all along I was on I–75. It never occurred to me that I was going the wrong way. The road I was on felt right to me. I'm sure there were signs and markers along the way indicating that I was on I–75, but they never got my attention. It never occurred to me that I might be going the wrong way. I had the radio turned up, and I was singing along to the music, completely oblivious. I never allowed for the possibility that I was on the wrong road.

In Matthew chapter 7 Jesus talks about two different roads that lead to different places:

> "Enter through the narrow gate. For wide is the gate and broad is the road that leads to destruction, and many enter through it. But small is the gate and narrow the road that leads to life, and only a few find it."
>
> Matthew 7:13–14

Many people take the wrong road, and only a few find the narrow path. If that is true, then wouldn't it make sense for us to slow down? Shouldn't we hit the brakes, pull over to the side, and make sure that we are on the road that leads to life? This teaching of Jesus is the conclusion of his sermon known as "The Sermon on the Mount." It's a sermon that is all about raising the bar of commitment for those who would follow him. It's a narrow road, but it's a road that leads to life.

I'm just wondering, is it possible that you think you are on the narrow road, but you are actually on the broad road? Could it be that you have set cruise control, turned up the Christian radio, and are traveling down the road of destruction with a Jesus fish on your bumper?

Donald Whitney once said, "If a person is wrong about being right with God, then ultimately it really doesn't matter what he or she is right about." So before you continue driving down the road, I'm just asking you to slow down the car and look at some of the signs and ask yourself what road you are on. Is it possible that you are wrong about being right with God? Jesus continues his teaching in Matthew 7:

> "Not everyone who says to me, 'Lord, Lord,' will enter the kingdom of heaven, but only the one who does the will of my Father who is in heaven. Many will say to me on that day, 'Lord, Lord, did we not prophesy in your name and in your name drive out

> demons and in your name perform many miracles?' Then I will tell them plainly, 'I never knew you. Away from me, you evildoers!'"
>
> MATTHEW 7:21–23

It wouldn't surprise me if Jesus said a *few* will stand before God on Judgment Day convinced that everything is fine only to find out otherwise. But he doesn't say *few*. He doesn't say *some*. He says *many*. Many who assumed they were on the path to heaven will find out that heaven is not their destination.

So if you've pulled the car over to the side of the road, I want you to ask yourself a couple of important questions from what Jesus teaches in Matthew 7.

Question 1: Does Your Life Reflect What You Say You Believe?

In verse 21 we read, "Not everyone who says . . . but only he who does . . ." Jesus makes a distinction between fans and followers by contrasting the word *says* with the word *does*. We live at a time when we have become increasingly comfortable with separating what we say we believe with how we live. We have convinced ourselves that our beliefs are sincere even if they have no impact on how we live. Let me give you a few examples of this mentality.

If I did a survey and asked Americans, "Do you believe it's important to eat right and exercise?" most all of them would say, "Yes, I believe that." Americans overwhelmingly say their health is important. But the most popular food at state fairs is a bacon cheeseburger with a bun made out of two Krispy Kreme donuts. You're charged extra if you want chocolate covered bacon.

Here's another example. A man might say, "I believe in the importance of family. Nothing matters more to me than my family." But if he turns around and accepts a higher paying job even though it will require more time away from his family, he has revealed what he really believes.

We are saved by God's grace when we believe in Jesus and put our faith in him, but biblical belief is more than something we confess with our mouths; it's something we confess with our lives.

So a fan may say "Lord, Lord," but a fan doesn't live "Lord, Lord." You say, "I am a follower." I hear you, but when is the last time you fed the hungry, clothed the naked, visited the prisoner? You say, "I am a follower." Well that's great, but what do you do when you get in an argument with your spouse? I want to know if you're the one who reaches over and puts a gentle hand on the back of your husband or wife and says, "I'm sorry." What do you do when a neighbor starts to gossip about a friend? What do you do when the movie you're watching continues to take God's name in vain? A belief is more than what we say.

The book of James in the Bible addresses this. James wants his readers to understand biblical belief:

> What good is it, my brothers and sisters, if someone claims to have faith but has no deeds? Can such faith save them? Suppose a brother or sister is without clothes and daily food. If one of you says to them, "Go in peace; keep warm and well fed," but does nothing about their physical needs, what good is it?
>
> JAMES 2:14–16

More Than a Feeling

Here's what fans tend to do: they confuse their feelings for faith. But your feelings aren't faith until they are expressed. This hit me in a very personal way a number of years ago. I was up late at night flipping through the channels, and I came across a program showing images of children with bloated stomachs who were malnourished and starving.

I laid there on my couch watching these heart-wrenching images. My eyes welled up with tears. My heart broke for those children. I was really moved. After a few minutes I got up from the couch, feeling pretty good about myself as a Christian; after all, not everyone would have such a sensitive heart towards the hurting. I felt something, but did nothing, and that's not biblical belief.

Faith is more than a feeling. Faith should have a story attached to it. There is a tendency to define yourself as a follower based on how you feel about Jesus, but following requires there to be more than a feeling. Following requires movement.

James concludes in verse 17:

> Faith by itself, if it is not accompanied by action, is dead.

When I was studying the word *belief*, I came across a secular article written by a psychiatrist. In the article he addressed the beliefs of his patients that had no basis in reality. A patient may sincerely believe he could fly—but that didn't mean anything because there was nothing to back that up. The patient might be an abusive husband who sincerely believes abuse is wrong—but he doesn't really believe that because his stated belief is contradicted by reality. But when the psychiatrist was speaking about his patients with beliefs that had no basis in reality, he didn't call them "beliefs." Do you know what he called them? He called them "delusions." We don't often think of it this way, but here's an important truth that needs some attention in circles of faith: a belief that's not reflected in reality isn't a belief at all; it's a delusion.

Question 2: Do You Think You're on the Right Road Because of What You've Done?

Just as dangerous as assuming that what we *say* alone shows that we are on the right road, is the assumption that what we *do* alone moves us down the narrow road. Notice the ways the fans defend themselves in Matthew 7. They will say to Jesus on that day, "We prophesied, we drove out demons, we performed miracles." Their confidence is in their righteous acts and their good deeds. One of the ways you know you're more fan than follower is that when I asked, "Are you a follower?" your mind immediately went to the fact that you go to church, put some money in the plate, and volunteer from time to time.

The hypothetical examples of righteousness that Jesus chooses in Matthew 7 are somewhat surprising. They seem pretty impressive from where I sit. I've never driven out demons or performed miracles. If they can't get in with their list, there's no way my list is going to get me into heaven. And I think that's exactly the point Jesus is trying to make. It seems that Jesus intentionally chooses the more dramatic and extraordinary spiritual achievements to make one thing clear: no matter how much good you do, no matter what you accomplish for the kingdom, that's not what makes you a true follower.

Ultimately the question that will identify you as a fan or follower isn't what you say or what you do. Those things matter, but only to the extent that they reflect the answer to this last question.

Question 3: Do I Know Jesus, and Does He Know Me?

That's what it comes down to in Matthew 7. That's the dividing line that Jesus identifies. In verse 23 he says to the fans, "I never knew you." So it comes down to a personal relationship with Jesus where you know him and are known by him. We want to put the emphasis on what we say and do. Those things are more measurable. They are tangible. We can point to them in the courtroom as evidence. But Jesus identifies his true followers based upon an intimate relationship. What we say and what we do overflows out of the relationship we have with him.

Just slow down for a moment and ask yourself: *Does Jesus know me?* Because a day is coming where many who have said the right things and done the right things will hear Jesus say, "Away from me. I never knew you."

Again, please understand, I'm not trying to make you paranoid. I believe what the Bible teaches about salvation. I believe that we are saved by the grace of God through faith in Jesus Christ (Eph. 2:8). I believe it is God alone who is able to keep us from falling (Jude 1:24). I believe that nothing can separate us from the love of God (Rom. 8:38–39). But I also believe the Bible clearly teaches that there will be those who think they are saved but who are not. They will live out their lives with a false assurance of salvation. They will think of themselves as followers, but a day will come when they'll be pronounced as nothing more than fans.

After I first preached this message, I had an experience with a new member of our church, a young single father. He had grown up in the church and made a decision for Jesus as a kid but had never really committed to him. But within a few months of coming to church he was all-in. He fell in love with Jesus. He had discovered the pearl of great price, and it was worth everything he had. The change in his life was pretty dramatic. His relationship with Jesus turned his life upside down. Before following Jesus, his life consisted, in his words, of "going out, drinking, smoking pot, and chasing girls." He'd show up to work with a hangover more often than not. He was full of anger and didn't know why. He felt like he was running in circles with no purpose, just going through life aimlessly. But following Jesus brought a radical change to his life. If you spend a few minutes with him, it's easy to see the joy that he has found in Christ. He is constantly at church, serving in whatever way he can. He's a single dad with plenty of financial struggles, but when he became a Christian he decided that he would no longer work during church times, even though he needed the hours. He started to give generously even though things were tight.

Not long ago he asked if I would have coffee sometime with him and his mom. I did not know his mom, but I said I would meet with them. When the three of us sat down for coffee I thought I knew what she wanted to talk to me about. I was aware that she went to a different church in town, and I assumed that she wanted to meet with me to say thank you. I thought she wanted to express appreciation for what was happening in her son's life. But that wasn't the case. She was upset with him. She blamed me and she blamed the church because she said, "My son has taken all of this too far." She was not pleased with how much time he was spending at the church. Some of the relatives were bothered by his desire to always want to pray before the family meals. He wouldn't be quiet about the sermons and was handing out CDs of the messages. She didn't think it was wise for him to give some of his hard-earned money to the church. And lately he had been talking about going on a mission trip. After she made her case that he had taken this all too far, with a tone of frustration she asked me, "Can you please tell him that the Bible teaches 'everything in moderation'? Can you please tell him that it doesn't have to be all or nothing?"

I tried to keep a pleasant smile, but my teeth were clenched, and my breath was short. I was feeling defensive of my friend. I could feel my eyebrows narrowing and saw my nostrils flare. So I did what I always do when I get angry; I started quoting Scripture from Revelation. I said to this lady who had been in church most of her life, "In Revelation 3 Jesus says to the Christians in Laodicea, 'because you are lukewarm—neither hot nor cold—I'm about to spit you out of my mouth.' Jesus doesn't say, 'everything in moderation'; he says you can't be my follower if you don't give up everything. His invitation is an all or nothing invitation."

Jesus has defined the relationship he wants with you. He is not interested in enthusiastic admirers who practice everything in moderation and don't get carried away. He wants completely committed followers.

PART TWO
An Invitation to Follow

SEVEN

Anyone—An Open Invitation

In the first section we identified where things stand in our relationship with Jesus. In this section we will discover where he wants to take us when we decide to follow him. These next few chapters will examine Jesus' invitation to follow him from Luke 9:23. In this passage Jesus clearly lays out his expectations of his followers. This verse defines the relationship Jesus wants to have. It spells out his terms so that we can know exactly what we are agreeing to when we make a decision to follow.

Anyone Means Everyone

In the New King James Version, Jesus begins his call to follow him with these two words, "*If anyone . . .*"

Anyone is a significant word because it makes it clear whom he is inviting. He is inviting *anyone*. *Anyone* is an all-inclusive word. *Anyone* means *everyone*. Jesus doesn't begin with a list of prequalifications. His invitation to follow is addressed to *anyone*. Many people don't realize they've been invited to follow. They think, *Not after what I've done. He wouldn't want me to follow him. I would never make the cut.* They assume they aren't qualified and as a result never take seriously what it means to follow Jesus. After all, what's the point in filling out an application if you know you won't get approved?

‣ ‣ ‣

A few years ago, my wife bought a white love seat to go in the room with the white carpet in our house. I should tell you we didn't put in the white carpet; it was the lovely decision of the childless couple who occupied the residence prior to us. So we had a white couch on white carpet. But my wife laid down the law and made sure that the kids knew they were not allowed in the "white room." It seemed to be working fine, until one day my wife was straightening up in that room, and she discovered a secret that someone had been keeping. She happened to flip over one of the couch cushions, and there was a stain. She called me into the room and showed me the pink fingernail polish blotched on the white cushion. She wasn't happy. We called our girls into the room. She had the cushion flipped back over so you couldn't see the stain. The interrogation was about to begin, but as I reached toward the cushion to expose the stain, my middle daughter Morgan cracked. She turned and ran up the steps.

▸ ▸ ▸

Most of us are hiding some stains. Our worst fear is that someone will flip the cushion over and discover what we've tried to hide. But because Jesus knows about our stains, we think that disqualifies us. Surely our stains get our names scratched off the invitation list to be a follower of Christ. He wouldn't want us.

If any of his closest followers felt that way it had to be Matthew. When we are first introduced to Matthew, he had stopped trying long ago to hide his stains. They were significant enough that it's highly probable that his family and friends had written him off. At the very least, he was a massive disappointment to his parents. They had very different plans for their son. We know this because Matthew had another name: Levi. To be given that name meant that your parents expected you to serve the Lord as the Levites of the Old Testament did. From birth, he was set aside to be a spiritual leader for the nation of Israel. Matthew's father, grandfather, and great-grandfather were likely all priests who served the Lord. By age twelve, Matthew would have had the first five books of the Bible memorized. It's likely that Matthew tried to become a disciple of one of the rabbis. But if he sent in his application, it was turned down. He didn't make the cut. Matthew flunked out of rabbi school. He couldn't measure up.

Whatever happened, we know that something had definitely gone wrong. Instead of serving the Lord, he decided to serve himself. He turned his back on his own people and became a tax collector for the Romans. Essentially his job description was to unfairly take money from his people and give it to the occupying Roman government. Even if he'd collected taxes fairly, he was working for the enemy. But in those days there was no such thing as an honest tax collector. They would cheat the people to line their own pockets. A tax collector was seen as a religious and social outcast. He was ceremonially unclean; he wasn't even allowed into the outer court of the tabernacle. His name had been scratched off the membership.

And you and me, we have a lot in common with Matthew. Maybe you're not stealing money from your neighbors, but we've all become disappointments. We haven't measured up; we haven't made the cut. The Bible says in Romans that all of us have sinned and fallen short of the glory of God. We've said things we shouldn't have said. We've done things we wish we wouldn't have done. And as hard as we have scrubbed the stain, it just won't come out.

I can't help but wonder if Matthew had chosen the life of a tax collector in an attempt to ignore the stains in his life. That can happen with poor choices, right? One mistake snowballs into the next, and eventually you think, *What's the point? Why even try anymore?* Whatever Matthew's past, he had reached a point where he was no longer even trying to hide it.

Every day Matthew sat at his tax collector booth on a busy street. As a boy growing up he never imagined it would come to this. In moments where he was honest with himself, maybe late at night staring up at the ceiling, he had to be full of guilt and regret. If only he could start over and do things differently. But what could he do now? His stains were set. They were never coming out.

▸ ▸ ▸

Just before I flipped over the cushion, Morgan turned and ran. She headed up the steps and hid.

I went after her. I called her name a few times. She didn't answer. I began to check the rooms and eventually found her in her closet with her head buried in her knees. I could hear her crying. She didn't want to look up. I got down in the closet with her and put my hand on her back. I wondered what she thought my response was going to be. Did she think I would get angry? Did she think I would yell? Was she afraid that I wouldn't love her? We went downstairs together, and she told her mom and me what happened. She let out the secret she had been keeping for months. She had spilled the fingernail polish, and then she tried to clean it up. She scrubbed and scrubbed, but the stain just got worse.

Eventually, she flipped the cushion over to hide what she had done. She said she had felt sick to her stomach every time we were in that room. She was scared that we would find out. And then she asked a question that melted us. She looked up with her big brown eyes full of tears and asked, "Do you still love me?"

▸ ▸ ▸

My guess is Matthew no longer asked that question. He couldn't imagine that God still wanted him. I'm sure Matthew had heard about a new rabbi on the scene. His name was Jesus, and he was doing things differently. And then one day, Matthew was at his tax collector's booth and Jesus stopped by and spoke to him. No one would have predicted what Jesus would say. It was only two words, but these two words changed everything for Matthew. Jesus said, "Follow me." A Jewish rabbi asking a tax collector for the Roman oppressors to be one of his followers? It's hard to overstate how unthinkable that scenario would have been for those close by.

It's important to understand what it meant in that culture for Jesus to be a rabbi. He may have been a homeless, unconventional rabbi, but he was a rabbi nonetheless. And a rabbi was a teacher of God's Word, which, at the time, was the Old Testament. Rabbis had extensive knowledge of the Torah (the first five books of the Bible) and all the writings of the prophets.

Rabbis were also special because they had a group of talmidim (pronounced *tal-mee-deem*). The word *talmid* translates to "disciple" or "student." So, essentially, every rabbi had a class of students, and this was an incredibly exclusive group. Most people didn't end up as students of rabbis. Those who didn't make the cut most often ended up learning some sort of trade, typically one that was passed down in their family.

For those students wanting to become the talmid of a particular rabbi, there was an application process. There were hefty prerequisites before even being considered. These were the equivalent of the GPA and transcript prerequisites for getting into an elite college or academy. If you want to go to Harvard, you better have a 4.0 GPA, or a 36 on your ACT, or a 1600 SAT score. Without those kinds of stats, you're probably not going to cut it. The same goes for a talmid applying to join a rabbi's school.

Talmidim had to have an impressive knowledge of Scripture, and a rabbi would quiz prospective talmidim, asking them to recite an entire book. Or they might ask a question like, "What is the number of times the name of the Lord is used in the eleventh chapter of Leviticus?" The selection was an intense, painstaking process. But rabbis had to be thorough, because the excellence of the student reflected the excellence of the teacher. The teacher was known for his students. If a rabbi just let in anyone, it would be clear that he was not a sought-after teacher. On the other hand, if a rabbi's group of talmidim were an especially brilliant and elite group, the rabbi would be respected and admired.

So the rabbis would take applications for followers. But that's not the way Rabbi Jesus went about getting followers. Instead of followers applying,

Jesus invited followers. This approach of going to someone and inviting him just wasn't done. A rabbi wouldn't humble himself or extend himself in that way. A rabbi wouldn't risk rejection; a rabbi would do the rejecting. But Jesus takes the initiative. It would have been shocking enough if he had simply allowed Matthew to follow him, but Jesus actually extends the invitation. He says to Matthew, "Follow me."

Anyone hearing this exchange would have been shocked. I'm sure the other disciples would have been offended. *A tax collector?* He's not only a sinner, he sins for a living. Jesus finds Matthew hiding behind this tax collector's booth, and when Jesus comes by, Matthew expects a pointed finger and words of rejection. Instead he finds open arms and a gracious invitation.

‣ ‣ ‣

Morgan asked, "Do you still love me?" My wife knelt down beside her on the floor, and she whispered to our daughter, *"Morgan, you could never make a big enough stain to keep me from loving you."* I wish I could tell you that somehow we were able to get the stain out and make the couch white again . . . but that stain is still there. It will always be there. But a funny thing happened. Morgan started telling the story of the stained white couch. She likes to show people the stain and tell them what happened. Why? Because a stain that once represented shame and guilt and fear of rejection now represents love, grace, and acceptance.

‣ ‣ ‣

Do you know how we know about Matthew's past as a tax collector? Do you know how we know that his friends were prostitutes, drunkards, and thieves? The reason we know all of that is because Matthew tells us. He calls us into the living room and shows us the stain on the couch and tells us the story of love and grace.

When Jesus invited Matthew to follow, he was making it clear that this is an invitation extended not solely to the religious elite, the morally upright, and those who have their lives together. It is an invitation to all of us who are hiding some stains. Jesus throws out the elitist application process and gives an open invitation.

Have you ever seen one of those car dealership commercials that advertises, "Anyone can buy a car here!" But if you look closely there is an asterisk next to that statement. At the bottom of the screen there is an asterisk with three letters: W.A.C. You know what W.A.C. stands for? With Approved Credit.

That's what they mean by *anyone.*

Anyone who meets the qualifications.

Anyone who makes it through the approval process.

When we read the word *anyone* in the invitation of Jesus, we can't help but think there must be an asterisk next to it. Even if there wasn't one when Jesus spoke these words, it seems that over the years the church has put an asterisk next to his invitation. The sign out front of the church says, *We welcome anyone and everyone.* But if you look closely, you'll find an asterisk. And it turns out that *anyone* means people who appear to have their lives together and don't have visible struggles. *Anyone* does not include those who struggle with addictions or who have gone through a divorce. *Anyone* means people who dress appropriately. *Anyone* means those from certain social and economic backgrounds who are affiliated with a certain political party and have a certain taste in music.

Recently I was sent the following letter from a lady in our church who told about an experience she had. Here's what she said:

> *It was about five minutes till the service started. A young woman, probably late twenties or early thirties, with her ten-year-old son approached me with a "deer in the headlights"*

look. She had never been here and was clearly anxious. I took her to the check-in counter for her son's class. On the way she told me that she had gotten divorced six years ago and after that she was no longer welcome at the church she had gone to. She hadn't been to church since then. You could hear the guilt and fear in her voice. She was terribly nervous. I shared with her that I had been divorced, and as a single mom I knew how tough it was. Once her son was in class I asked her if she wanted to sit with me in worship. Upon hearing my invitation she asked, "Am I allowed to go inside there?" She pointed to the sanctuary. I told her she was.

When we got to our seats the service had already started, and everyone was standing and singing. After the song the worship leader prayed, and the first words out of his mouth were, "God, thank you that no matter where our path has taken us in life, you can redeem and forgive us." With that, her tears started to flow and really didn't stop throughout the entire service. I could just see the fear and guilt melt away. At the end of the service you offered an invitation and asked anyone who wanted to talk more about surrendering his or her life to

> *Christ to come down front and meet you. Then we stood for the closing worship songs. Towards the end of the first song she appeared a bit antsy, and I assumed that she was probably ready to go get her son and head to the car. I turned to ask her if she was ready to leave, but before I had a chance she opened her mouth first and said, "Do I need to walk down there and talk to him if I want to make that decision?" I told her that would be a good place to start. She simply said, "I want to do that." I asked her if she wanted me to walk with her and she said, "Yes." So, we walked down front.*

I can tell you the rest of the story from there. I greeted her down front and saw the tears in her eyes. She leaned in to whisper in my ear, "I don't know if I'm allowed to respond to the invitation. I went through a divorce a number of years ago, and my old church wouldn't have me." She was stopped at the gate and told she didn't have the right qualifications. The cushion got flipped and someone decided her stain was too big.

Jesus has invited anyone to follow him, but when they come to church they find that there is an asterisk. The not-so-subtle message is: *We have to let you in here because Jesus told us to, but we are going to be keeping an eye on you*. I can't help but wonder if that's how the other disciples must have felt when Jesus invited Matthew. *What about his qualifications? What about his past history? Jesus, surely you don't really mean anyone?* But when Jesus says *anyone*, it turns out what he really means is anyone.

So there Matthew sat at his tax collector's booth, mulling over this rabbi's offer. There is no doubt that Matthew knew what this invitation involved. He understood that it meant giving up everything. He received an invitation, but there was no way he could respond to it and stay the same. Saying yes to following Jesus would mean saying no to his lucrative business.

Anyone can follow, but not without giving up everything.

Jesus says,

"Follow me."

Mathew 9:9 simply says:

. . . and Matthew got up and followed him.

These days, people don't know Matthew as a failure and embarrassment who sold his soul to the Romans for a job. They know Matthew as a follower of Jesus who wrote the first book of the New Testament.

It's important to understand that the grace of God doesn't simply invite us to follow . . . it teaches us to follow. Just because Matthew left his past behind and started following didn't mean he was perfect. Far from it. Even after we decide to follow Jesus, we continue to need his grace for the journey. There are plenty of days where I find myself living as a fan, but each morning I receive the same grace-filled invitation that Jesus spoke to Matthew: "Follow me."

So who is invited to follow Jesus? *Anyone.*
Sexual past? *Anyone.*
Ex-con? *Anyone.*
Current con? *Anyone.*
Recently divorced? *Anyone.*
Republican? Democrat? *Anyone.*
Alcoholic? *Anyone.*
Pothead? *Anyone.*
Addict? *Anyone.*
Hypocrite? *Anyone.*

I wonder if you've had a moment like Morgan—a moment like Matthew. The cushion gets flipped. The stain is exposed. You're guilty. You know what you deserve. You know what you have coming. But the words of Jesus are words full of grace. He says, "Follow me." You think, *There must be a mistake. Doesn't he know who I am? Doesn't he know what I've done?* Yeah, he knows about the stains. In fact, he died on the cross so that our stains could be washed clean, whiter than snow. And because of his grace, we find ourselves at the same crossroads as Matthew.

The invitation of Jesus to follow him begins, "If anyone . . ."

It turns out that *anyone* means *anyone*.

Anyone means me. *Anyone* means you.

EIGHT

Come after Me—A Passionate Pursuit

The next part of Jesus' invitation to follow him in Luke 9 will make complete sense to followers but will seem a bit crazy to the fans. In Luke 9:23 Jesus defines the relationship he wants with us. He makes it clear what it means to be a follower:

> "If anyone desires to come after Me, let him deny himself, and take up his cross daily, and follow Me" (NKJV).

The phrase I want to draw your attention to is *come after*. It's a phrase that was commonly used in the context of a romantic relationship. When Jesus says *come after*, he's describing a passionate pursuit of someone you love. So the best way to understand what Jesus is wanting from us as followers is to compare how we pursue him to how we would pursue someone with whom we want to have a romantic relationship. Most of us have done some illogical and irrational things in the passionate pursuit of someone we love. It's a pursuit that can easily consume our thoughts, our resources, and our energy. That's what Jesus is looking for from a follower when he says *come after.*

Crazy Love Stories

In our world, the relationship we tend to be the most passionate about pursuing is a romantic relationship. We are surrounded by messages that emphasize romantic love as the ultimate human experience. Pursuing love is the subject of countless books. It has inspired beautiful works of poetry and art. It's the plot line of innumerable movies. It is the theme of most every song. Who can forget Whitney Houston singing "I Will Always Love You" or Celine Dion singing "My Heart Will Go On"? Even if you would like to forget, it's difficult. The Beatles sang "And I Love Her." Stevie Wonder declared "You Are the Sunshine of My Life." And then there's that classic from Meatloaf, "I'd Do Anything for Love." He sings about just how far he would go to pursue that love. "*I would do anything for love. I'd run right into hell and back. I would do anything for love . . . But I won't do that . . .*" I never knew what "that" was . . . I won't do what? Share the remote, put down the toilet lid, pluck my eyebrows, change my name—I'm not sure what Meatloaf wouldn't do. But he would do a lot for love. He was willing to run right into hell and back.

Pursuing a romantic love will make us do some crazy things. When I was dating my soon-to-be wife, she borrowed my car to go visit her family about eighty miles away from where we went to college. She had only been gone for a day, but I missed her and wanted to be with her. I woke up in the middle of the night and couldn't stop thinking about her. I wanted to see her and tell her I loved her. I had to do something. My college roommate was sleeping in the bed across the room. I woke him up and told him my dilemma, but he couldn't do much to help because he didn't have a car. Suddenly, I had what seemed like a brilliant idea. I said to him, "What if we just ride bikes over to her house?"

He was up for it, but this new plan presented us with a similar problem as before: neither of us owned bikes. Then my buddy reminded me of the bike racks on campus. We decided it would be fine to "borrow" the bikes for our journey.

Knowing nothing about bicycles, I grabbed the first one I saw, which happened to be a Walmart special. It turns out this is not the bike of choice for an eighty-mile journey down the flat roads of Kansas against constant headwind. After riding for hours, we decided to park our bikes and take a nap in a ditch on the side of the road. While we were sleeping, a state trooper saw us and pulled over to investigate. He woke me up by placing his boot on my shoulder and jostling me awake. I believe his exact words were, "Are you boys smokin' something? What are you doing riding bikes across Kansas?"

I tried to explain: "I wanted to be with my fiancée." He rolled his eyes, shook his head, got in his car, and drove away. He thought I was crazy for doing such a thing.

When we finally made it, my wife's response was fairly similar to the state trooper's. She thought I was nuts. But the moment I saw her I knew it was worth it.

I could probably tell you a half dozen other stories of how I pursued my wife. I could tell you how I delivered furniture in the heat of the summer for minimum wage, but enjoyed it because the money was going to a wedding ring. I could tell you of the time in college I pulled an all-nighter to finish the research for a thirty-page research paper that she needed to turn in. I could tell you how I donated plasma so I could buy her a dozen roses. It's easy to get mushy and nostalgic looking back at the course of our relationship. I've spent so much energy chasing after her, so much time winning her heart, and I wouldn't trade it for anything. But you know, looking back at my relationship with Christ, I don't have as many stories about chasing after Jesus. The ones I could tell you hardly seem impressive enough to write down here.

Followers should have some *come after* Jesus stories that make people say, "That's crazy." Many fans didn't grow up thinking about their relationship with Jesus in these terms. Following him was more of a casual weekend thing. You didn't get too carried away with it. You might have thrown a few bucks in the offering and volunteered to hand out bulletins, but that was about the extent of it. And honestly, that is as far as you wanted it to go. But that's not how Jesus has defined the relationship.

Jesus wants us to understand that following him is a pursuit that requires everything we have. Jesus tells a parable in Matthew 13 called "The Pearl of Great Price." It gives us a picture of what Jesus had in mind when he invited us to *come after* him.

> "The kingdom of heaven is like treasure hidden in a field. When a man found it, he hid it again, and then in his joy went and sold all he had and bought that field."
>
> MATTHEW 13:44

In Bible times people would often bury their savings in the ground. It was considered a safe place, especially during times of war or government upheaval. It would not have been uncommon for someone to bury their treasure in the ground and then be killed while away at war. Jesus describes a scenario where years later a hired hand discovers a buried treasure chest while plowing. He stops, digs it up, brushes it off, and opens the lid. He can't believe his eyes! There are thousands of dollars' worth of precious gems glistening in the sun. His heart pounds with excitement. He quickly reburies the treasure and continues working, but the whole time he is carefully plotting his course of action. He is desperate to buy that field so the treasure will be his. That evening he liquidates his assets. He sells everything—his house, his oxen, his cart. Friends and family begin to talk. They think he's lost his mind. It just doesn't make sense. But the truth is, this is the best investment that he could possibly make.

When we discover the life that we can have in

Jesus, we are to come after him like this man pursued this pearl of great price. Fans are careful not to get carried away. Followers understand that following Jesus is a pursuit that may cost them everything, but it is the best investment they could ever make. Followers will do some crazy things for love, but fans want to play it safe.

In the parable of "The Pearl of Great Price" the man sold everything he had to get the treasure, but once he had the treasure did you notice his response? "Then in his joy [he] went and sold all he had and bought that field." Sacrificing everything he had for the treasure brought him great joy because he knew it was worth it.

Pursuing Jesus is your choice, and Jesus wants to make it clear what you're agreeing to if you respond to his invitation. He will settle for nothing less than to be the great love and pursuit of your life. That's what he wants. At church, we sometimes talk about how "God wants your time," or "God wants your money," or "God wants your worship." But do you understand why we talk about those things?

It's not because God *needs* your time. He has always been and always will be. It's not because he *needs* your money. He owns the cattle on a thousand hills. If God needed your money, he could take it. It's not that God *needs* your worship. If you don't worship, the Bible says that the rocks and trees will cry out. The reason we talk about those things is not because God needs or wants those things; it's because he wants *you*. He wants your love. He longs for you to passionately pursue him, and all those things are *come after* indicators.

One of the greatest motivations of our love and passionate pursuit of Jesus is a better understanding of how great his love is for us. Being loved causes us to love. We read in 1 John 4:19:

> We love Him because He first loved us (NKJV).

The craziest *come after* story of all is when God put on flesh, came to this earth, and died in our place. He took the initiative and pursued you. When we realize the extravagance of his love, it begins to change our hearts. We love him because he first loved us.

When I was back in my hometown visiting my family, I went with my grandma to visit the gravesite where my grandpa was buried. Next to his grave marker was a place reserved for my grandmother. It already had her name on it and the day of her birth. The date of her death will one day be added. If you asked her, she would say she is ready for that day right now. She hasn't been the same since my grandpa died. They were married almost sixty years. She misses him so much.

We stood in front of his gravesite, and she talked about feeling lonely. She told me she still reaches over for him at night. Sometimes she finds herself calling to him in the other room, just out of habit. We stood in silence for a few moments, and then she said this: "I'm ready. I'm ready to go home and be with . . ." and I knew what she was going to say next. She was going to say ". . . your grandpa." Of course she was going to say that. He was the love of her life. She loved him more than she loved anything. But she didn't say, "I'm ready to go home and be with your grandpa." What she said was, "I'm ready to go home and be with Jesus."

That's the heart of a follower.

NINE

Deny—A Total Surrender

I was at the gym last summer on one of the elliptical machines that faces the window. I was looking out at the parking lot and watching the people come in for a workout before heading home for the day. After a few minutes a guy pulled up and got out of his car. He was a large guy, and it took some effort for him to get out of his small sedan. He was still in his office clothes, but I watched as he reached in to grab his gym bag. He put it over his shoulder and then leaned into the car one more time to get something else. He emerged with a cup that had a red spoon in it. You get what's happening? This man was finishing off his Blizzard from Dairy Queen as he walked into the gym for his workout. He stood right outside the window in front of me to take his final bites. I'm pretty sure it was cookie dough. He threw the empty cup in the trash and walked in for his workout. He wanted to get in shape, but he didn't want to make any personal sacrifices.

That's how a fan will try and follow Jesus. A fan will try and accept the invitation of Christ to follow, but they don't want to say no to themselves. In Luke 9:23 Jesus makes it clear that if we are going to follow him, a casual no-strings-attached arrangement isn't a possibility:

> "If anyone desires to come after Me, let him deny himself . . ." (NKJV)

You can't come after Jesus without denying yourself. The phrase *deny himself* isn't just the idea of saying no to yourself—or even resisting yourself. The idea here is that you do not even acknowledge or recognize your own existence.

We talk a lot about the truth that being a Christian means believing in Jesus—but we don't say much about denying ourselves. That is such an unappealing message. How do you deny yourself in a culture that says it's all about you?

In Matthew chapter 19 we meet a man whose name we don't know. We learn enough about him from the Gospels that he is referred to as the "Rich Young Ruler." He's followed a path that has led to wealth and power. That's the path that most of us are trying to find. He comes to Jesus with a question. In verse 16 he asks:

> "Teacher, what good thing must I do to get eternal life?"

You have to give him credit for asking the right question. He wants to know, *How do I get to heaven?* But even the way he asks it reveals the heart of a fan. He says, what must I *do*. That word could be translated *acquire* or *earn*. He thinks it's going to be an impressive resume that will get him in. Eventually Jesus tells this man what he needs to do. In verse 21 Jesus says:

> "Sell your possessions and give to the poor, and you will have treasure in heaven. Then come, follow me."

Jesus invites the man to become his follower, but first the man is told to sell all his possessions and give to the poor. He's faced with the choice of following Jesus or keeping his stuff. He can't do both. There's no way to follow Jesus without denying himself.

Many people want to make this story about

money, but it's not as much about money as it is about following Jesus. Jesus puts this man at a crossroads. He can follow the path that leads to money, or he can follow Jesus, but he can't follow both.

So what does all this mean for you and me? Is selling everything a requirement to follow Jesus? Well, it may be. In fact, I would say, the more defensive you are of Jesus' words to this man, the more likely it is that Jesus might be saying them to you. What is true is that everyone who follows Jesus will find himself or herself at a similar crossroads as this man in Matthew 19. You won't be able to take the path of following Jesus without walking away from a different path. He wanted to follow Jesus, but when forced to choose between Jesus and his stuff, he chose his stuff. He wouldn't deny himself. What choice will you make?

Followers are willing to deny themselves and say, "I choose Jesus. I choose Jesus over my family. I choose Jesus over money. I choose Jesus over career goals. I am his completely. I choose Jesus over getting drunk. I choose Jesus over looking at porn. I choose Jesus over a redecorated house. I choose Jesus over my freedom. I choose Jesus over what other people may think of me." A follower makes a decision every day to deny himself and choose Jesus . . . even if it costs everything.

No Exception Clause

One way fans try to follow Jesus without denying themselves is by compartmentalizing the areas of their lives they don't want him to have access to. They try and negotiate the terms of the deal. *I'll follow Jesus, but I'm not going to sell my possessions. Don't ask me to forgive the people who hurt me; they don't deserve that. Don't ask me to save sex for marriage; I can't help my desires. Don't ask me to give a percentage of my money; I worked hard for that cash.* And instead of following Jesus with their financial life, they follow *Money* magazine. In their relationships, instead of Jesus they follow Oprah. In their sex lives, instead of following Jesus, they follow *Cosmo.*

Jesus never left open the option of selective commitment. There are no exception clauses. You don't get to say, "I follow Jesus—but when it comes to this area of my life, I do things my way." If you call yourself a Christian, by definition you are committing to following Christ with every area of your life. It doesn't mean you will follow perfectly, but you can't say, "I'm a Christian" and then refuse to follow Christ when it comes to certain people or places or practices.

I saw a report on MSNBC about a group of

new vegetarians. They interviewed one of the new vegetarians, a twenty-eight-year-old named Christy Pugh. One of her quotes captures the viewpoint of this group. She said, "I usually eat vegetarian. But I really like sausage." She represents a growing number of people who eat vegetarian but make some exceptions. They don't eat meat, unless they really like it. As you can imagine, the real vegetarians aren't very happy about the new vegetarians. They put pressure on the new vegetarians to change their name. And so here's the name they've chosen for themselves: flexetarians. As I watched the report I realized something: I'm a flexetarian. I absolutely refuse to eat meat, unless it's being served. Christy explains it this way, "I really like vegetarian food, but I'm just not a hundred percent committed."

"Flexetarian" is a good way to describe how many people approach their commitment to Christ. And that's the way many Christians approach their commitment to Jesus and the Bible. *I really like Jesus—but I don't really like serving the poor—but I'm not big into the idea of going to church—but my resources are spoken for. I love Jesus, but don't ask me to save sex for marriage. I love Jesus, but don't ask me to forgive the person who hurt me. I love Jesus, but I'm not a hundred percent committed.* They call themselves Christians.

They follow Jesus, but they've made some exceptions. So when bacon is on the menu, their commitments can be adjusted.

Following Jesus requires a complete and total commitment. What the Rich Young Ruler is really committed to is revealed when he refuses to deny himself. He wants to say yes to following Jesus without saying no to himself. He wants to be close enough to Jesus to have eternal life, but not so close that it requires personal sacrifice.

There is a legal document called a "quitclaim deed." It's used when a person is signing over all rights to property or a possession that they once had a share in. When they sign a quitclaim deed, they are giving up whatever claim they once had. They are surrendering all their rights. When Jesus invites us to follow, there's not a lot of paper work involved, but he's looking for some kind of a quitclaim deed. When you decide to follow him, you are signing over your house, your car, your bank accounts, your career, your marriage, your children, your future, and anything else that you once laid claim to. You have no more rights, and nothing can be withheld. You deny yourself and sign a quitclaim deed on your life.

Millard Fuller tells of becoming a millionaire

by the age of twenty-nine. He had, he says, bought his wife everything she could possibly want. But one day he came home to a note that announced that she had left him. Millard went after her. He found her on a Saturday night in a hotel in NYC. They talked into the wee hours of the morning as she poured out her heart and made him see that the "things" that our society says are supposed to be so satisfying had left her cold. Her heart was empty, and her spirit was burned out. She was dead inside, and she wanted to live again. Kneeling at their bedside in that hotel room, Millard and Linda decided to sell everything they had and dedicate themselves to serving poor people.

The next day being Sunday, they found the nearest Baptist church and went there to worship and thank God for their new beginning. They shared with the minister and told him about what had happened to them and the decision they had made. Ironically, the minister told them that such a radical decision was not really necessary. Millard said, "He told us that it was not necessary to give up everything. He didn't understand that we weren't just giving up money and the things that money could buy. We were giving up period." Millard and Linda started an organization you're probably familiar with—Habitat for Humanity.

That's what the story of the Rich Young Ruler is really about. It's not just about giving up money and the things that money can buy; it's about giving up, period. That's what it means to deny yourself and follow Christ.

TEN

Take up Your Cross Daily—An Everyday Death

When I was twenty-one years old, my wife and I moved to Los Angeles County, California, to start a new church. I read as much as I could about planting a church, but I had no experience and was in way over my head. I filled a notebook with questions about how to go about starting a new church. What seemed clear to me was that if a new church is to be successful, then people have to come. The more people that come = the more successful the church will be was such an obvious equation, I decided that there was only one question that really needed to be answered: How do I get as many people as possible to come to this new church?

The answer to this question soon led me into

reading some business books that were all about marketing your product and attracting customers. And without making a conscious decision to do so, I set out to start a new church like a person would start a new business.

I learned that when starting a new business, it's important to sit down and put together a business plan. Part of a good business plan is putting together a marketing strategy. A good marketing strategy relies upon, among other things, a slogan and a symbol that will attract potential customers. You want them to see your symbol and hear your slogan and think to themselves, *That's what I've been looking for—I want to be a part of that.*

The right slogan can not only bring your company to a customer's mind, but also create desire for the product. The symbol, or logo, of the company should be memorable and appealing. Here are a few examples of some famous slogans:

- Melts in your mouth, not in your hand.
- It's everywhere you want to be.
- Just do it.
- It keeps going, and going, and going . . .

Chances are you know most of those companies (in order: M&M's, Visa, Nike, Energizer) and have been, or at least would like to be, associated with them in some way. Not only do you know their names; my guess is you would be able to picture the symbol that represents each of those companies. The symbols represent fulfillment, pleasure, satisfaction, victory, style, and status. Those companies have worked hard to develop a slogan and a symbol that will be appealing and attract as many people as possible.

With that in mind, what would you identify as the slogan and symbol for followers of Christ? Jesus lays it out in Luke 9:23 when he extends an invitation to follow him.

> "If anyone desires to come after Me, let him deny himself, and take up his cross daily, and follow Me" (NKJV).

The slogan for followers of Christ could accurately be captured this way:

Come and die.

Well, at least it gets your attention. Not really the kind of slogan that draws people in. It sounds like a horror flick that is released around Halloween. It's not a slogan people flock to; it's a slogan people flee from. Nobody wants to talk about death. We don't even like the word *death.* When someone dies we say, *"They've passed on . . . they've gone ahead . . . they're no longer with us . . . they've kicked the bucket . . . they've bought the farm . . . they're pushing up daisies . . . they're swimmin' with the fish."* Death is so final; it's so complete. Exactly. As Bonhoeffer put it, "When Christ calls a man, he bids him come and die."

The symbol for followers of Christ isn't any better. It is a cross. An instrument of torture and death is the image that represents followers of Jesus.

It seems like there were other options that Jesus could have gone with. Why not a dove? It represents peace. What about a shepherd's staff? It's a symbol of protection. Or a rainbow; it represents hope and promise. Why choose two bloody beams nailed together? If you want to attract customers, an image of perhaps the most brutal means of execution ever devised isn't a great place to start.

We've tried to make the most of it. We've turned it into ornaments and pieces of jewelry. But to those who were hearing these words of Jesus in Luke 9, the invitation to take up a cross would have been both offensive and repulsive.

For the Jews, the cross was a means of execution that the Romans used to force them into submission. It was a symbol of the Romans' power and strength. Every once in a while a group of Jewish rebels would rise up and lead a revolt against the Roman oppression. The Romans would crucify those involved in the rebellion, sometimes crucifying as many as two thousand at a time along the dusty roads of Palestine.

The cross was a symbol of humiliation. In the ancient world, the Romans had a number of ways to carry out an execution. They knew how to execute people very cheaply. Some people would be executed by fire, and others would be stoned. Still others would be killed with a stroke of the sword. They might simply give a person a drink of hemlock. Crucifixion, on the other hand, required four soldiers and a centurion to oversee. It was much more expensive. So why crucifixion? They would use it when they wanted to publicly humiliate the person being crucified. They wanted to make a public statement that this person had no power and was nothing. We read in Scripture how the soldiers humiliated and mocked Jesus. They spit on him. The Bible says he was crucified *naked* on a cross.

Here was Jesus, the Creator, the Savior, and the King of Kings. The one who had everything made himself nothing. He, who had the world at his feet, chose to come and wash the feet of the world. If we are going to follow him, it means humbly taking up a cross and making ourselves nothing.

There is no comfortable way to carry a cross; I don't care how you position it. I often talk to people who are convinced that some suffering or pain in their lives is an indication that they must not be following Jesus. After all, if they are following Jesus, the Son of God, doesn't it follow that things in life are going to unfold smoothly? There is this junk theology floating around out there that points to difficulties as evidence that you must not be following Jesus. The biblical reality is that when people say yes to following Jesus, they are agreeing to carry a cross, and that will be painful at times.

There are a number of Scriptures that do more than hint at the fact that following Jesus will cost you something.

> Luke 6:22: "Blessed are you when people hate you, when they exclude you and insult you and reject your name as evil, because of the Son of Man."
>
> 2 Timothy 3:12: Everyone who wants to live a godly life in Christ Jesus will be persecuted.
>
> Philippians 1:29: For it has been granted to you on behalf of Christ not only to believe on him, but also to suffer for him.

And here's the question that is keeping me awake these days: *Am I really carrying a cross if there is no suffering and sacrifice?* When is the last time that following Jesus cost you something? When is the last time it cost you a relationship? When is the last time following Jesus cost you a promotion? When is the last time it cost you a vacation? When is the last time you were mocked for your faith? When is the last time you went without a meal for the sake of the gospel? Can you really say you are carrying your cross if it hasn't cost you anything? Take a second and answer that question in your mind. Has it cost you anything? If there is no sacrifice involved, if you're not at least a little uncomfortable, then there is a good chance that you aren't carrying a cross.

Ultimately the cross was a symbol of death. When Jesus got to Golgotha, the place of the skull, the soldiers took the horizontal beam and attached it to the vertical beam to make a cross. His hands were nailed to the tree. Next the soldiers nailed Jesus' feet to the cross. Hours later a spear was thrust into his side to confirm his death. Jesus invites followers to die to themselves. We die to our own desires, our pursuits, and our plans. When we become followers of Jesus, that is the end of us.

A cross, more than anything else, represents death. For those carrying a cross the outcome is certain. "Dead man walking" is a phrase sometimes used to describe a person on death row, and the expression is certainly appropriate for a follower carrying a cross. Jesus takes the most despised and rejected symbol of his time and says, "If you want to follow me, take this up." He invites us to die.

Jesus makes it clear that following him means taking up your cross and dying to yourself. That's what a follower is committing to. Unfortunately, many churches today have decided that this message is too uncomfortable, and the cross is too offensive. As a result, there are many fans who call themselves followers, but they're not carrying a cross.

Snuggie Theology

Contrast the symbol of the cross with our love for comfort. Most of us commit our time and our resources to making our lives as comfortable as possible. We are by nature comfort seekers, not cross bearers. We are the people of the La-Z-Boy, the country club, the day spa, and the Snuggie. Contrast the image of the Snuggie with the image of the cross. One represents ease and comfort; the other represents pain and sacrifice. Unfortunately, many churches have developed Snuggie Theology, where they try and make sure everyone is as comfortable as possible. The Snuggie Theology promises health and wealth to all who follow Jesus. Instead of promising you a cross to carry, they promise you a luxury car and a beautiful home. The message may still be preached from the Bible in a church, but certain parts are left out, and if you look around my guess is that you won't see any crosses in the building.

You start to see the consequences of the Snuggie Theology when someone's health takes a turn for the worse or their finances begin to fall apart. They start to question God, because according to the gospel that was presented to them, God isn't holding up his end of the deal. One of the elders at our church described in a sentence how this happens. He said, *"What you win them with is what you win them to."* When we win them with Snuggie Theology, they are not going to be happy when they are told to take up a cross.

Jesus didn't come to this earth to tweak your personality or fine-tune your manners or smooth out your rough spots. Jesus didn't even come to this earth to change you. The truth of the gospel is that Jesus came so that you could die.

In *Mere Christianity* C. S. Lewis puts it this way:

> *Christ says, "Give me all. I don't want so much of your time and so much of your money and so much of your work: I want you. I have not come to torment your natural self, but to kill it. No half-measures are any good. I don't want to cut off a branch here and a branch there. I*

> *want to have the whole tree down. I don't want to drill the tooth, or crown it, or stop it, but to have it out."*

The slogan is "Come and die," and the symbol is the cross.

I've been around my share of dead people. I've been in the room before the coroner comes in. I have stood next to many open caskets as friends and family walked by to say goodbye. And I don't mean to be uncouth, but I've noticed something about dead people. People who are dead don't seem to care very much what other people think of them. Dead people aren't concerned with how nice their clothes are. Dead people aren't caught up in how much money is in their account. Dead people aren't at all thinking about getting the promotion. The point is that death is the ultimate surrender of yourself and all that you have. When you're dead, you're no longer concerned with your life.

Dying Daily

Jesus invites you to "*take up your cross . . .*" That is often where we leave his invitation. But it's the next word that makes all the difference. The word is *daily*. Take up your cross daily. Dying to ourselves is not a one-time decision. It's a daily decision. That's the most challenging part of dying.

In my closet where I get on my knees each morning and surrender to Jesus, I have three words spray-painted on the wall. They are Paul's words found in 1 Corinthians 15:31. Paul says:

> I die daily. (NKJV)

That's the hardest part of carrying your cross . . . it's daily. Each morning by the grace of Jesus, I am invited to take up a cross and die. That's the only way I will follow him that day. Every morning we crawl back on the altar and die to ourselves. That's Jesus' invitation in Luke 9:23, but look at what he says in the very next verse:

> "For whoever wants to save their life will lose it, but whoever loses their life for me will save it."

It's only by dying to ourselves that we truly find life. When we finally let go of our lives, we find real life in Christ. Those of you who have experienced this understand what Jesus is saying. For some of the fans, none of this makes sense. In fact, in 1 Corinthians 1:18 Paul wrote . . .

> For the message of the cross is foolishness to those who are perishing, but to us who are being saved it is the power of God.

One version puts it this way, "The message about the cross doesn't make any sense . . ." (CEV). Dying to yourself doesn't make sense to the fan, but the follower understands that dying is the secret of really living.

The cross that represented defeat—for a follower it is an image of victory.
The cross that represented guilt—for a follower it is an image of grace.
The cross that represented condemnation—for a follower it is an image of freedom.
The cross that represented pain and suffering—for a follower it is an image of healing and hope.
The cross that represented death—for a follower it is an image of life.
The cross may not be attractive, but for a follower it is beautiful.

Taking up a cross and dying to myself sounds like torture. We think that such a decision would make us miserable. But when we die to ourselves and completely surrender to him, there is a surprising side effect to dying: we discover true life. In a twist of irony, we find that giving up our lives gives us the life we so desperately wanted all along.

PART THREE
Following Jesus

ELEVEN

Wherever. *What about There?*

> "If anyone desires to come after Me,
> let him deny himself, and take up
> his cross daily, and follow Me."
> LUKE 9:23 NKJV

When you read this invitation there is a tendency to read it as being poetic. Even as we break it down word for word, the dramatic and radical nature of the invitation tends to draw an emotional response. But as you step across the line and commit to being a follower, it's important to understand and think through the personal and more practical implications.

At the end of Luke chapter nine, after Jesus offers an invitation to follow him, we are introduced to three people who initially seem eager to be followers. However, as they process how following Jesus will impact their specific situations, they begin making excuses. As they try to negotiate the terms of their commitment to Jesus, it becomes clear that they're really just fans.

We meet the first of these fans in verse 57. He approaches Jesus and his disciples:

> As they were walking along the road, a man said to him, "I will follow you wherever you go."

Those words certainly sound impressive. He seems to understand what Jesus was looking for. He knows the right words to say. He states his commitment to Jesus and says, *"I will follow you wherever you go."* Wherever. That sure sounds like a follower. No restrictions. No boundaries. No borders. Wherever. But look at verse 58:

> Jesus replied, "Foxes have dens and birds have nests, but the Son of Man has no place to lay his head."

Jesus turns to this man and says, "Hey bro, I'm homeless." My guess is that this revelation was often a deal breaker for a lot of would-be followers. Jesus is making it clear up front that following him won't mean going from town to town staying at the Ritz and ordering room service.

The man says, *"I will follow you wherever."* And Jesus points to a place that will be a threat to this man's comfort and security and asks, *"What about there?"* We're left with the impression that this wannabe follower quickly rescinded his offer. *"Did I say wherever? That was meant to be more of a poetic expression. Figuratively speaking, I will follow you wherever."*

It's much easier to speak about following Jesus when you are making a general statement without any specific commitments. But the most obvious and basic definition of following Jesus means that you go where Jesus goes. When you think of it that way, suddenly those poetic words have some huge implications.

Like this first man, we may be quick to say to Jesus, *"I will follow you wherever . . ."* But let's move it from the general to the more specific. Where is the one place you find it most difficult to follow Jesus? If you said to Jesus *"Wherever,"* where do you think is the one place he would point to and say, *"What about there?"*

Wherever? What about in your own home?

There is the tendency to carry a cross and follow Jesus, but before we walk in the door of our own home, we leave the cross on the front porch.

Instead of submitting, you stand up for your rights. Instead of serving, you sit around. Instead of being patient, you are demanding. Instead of being encouraging, you are constantly critical. Instead of being a spiritual leader, you are passive and apathetic in your own home. So what about *there*?

Wherever? What about at work? At 9 a.m. during the week, you'll find many fans getting out of their cars and saying to Jesus, *"You wait here. I'll be back to get you around five."* When they clock in to work, they clock out of following.

They justify greed by calling it ambition. They rationalize dishonesty by calling it shrewd business. They stay quiet about their faith at work and call it being tolerant.

I received an email from a lady who asked me to pray for her because she wanted to take seriously this challenge of following Jesus anywhere. Though she had worked in the same small office for seven years, no one knew she was a Christian or went to church. She decided that she needed to start being bolder about her faith. There was a coworker who had the space next to her. Over the years they had become good friends, but she had never talked about her faith in God. Her plan was to invite her coworker to a special event we were having at the church and to talk to her that night about her faith. A few weeks after I received the email I hadn't heard anything and wondered how things had turned out. She wrote back and said it was a really embarrassing and convicting moment for both of them. She went to her friend and invited her to church, and her friend laughed and said, "That's where I go to church, and I was going to invite you." What initially struck them as funny quickly made them feel sick. For seven years they'd worked next to each other, and neither of them had realized the other was a Christian. They both called themselves followers, but they weren't following at work. So what about *there*?

Wherever? What about at the game? What about in the neighborhood? What about when you're back home with old friends? Or what if God points to a place like Burma or Thailand and says, *"What about there?"*

Anne Judson was the wife of America's first foreign missionary, Adoniram Judson. Adoniram was twenty-four when he decided to leave America and sail to Burma. Burma didn't have a single missionary and was an extremely hostile environment. He was in love with Anne, who was twenty-three at the time. Adoniram wanted to marry Anne and then move to Burma to spread the gospel. Before he married Anne, he wrote her father the following letter asking for her hand in marriage:

> *I have now to ask, whether you can consent to part with your daughter early next spring, to see her no more in this world; whether you can consent to her departure, and her subjection to the hardships and sufferings of missionary life; whether you can consent to her exposure to the dangers of the ocean, to the fatal influence of the southern climate of India; to every kind of want and distress; to degradation, insult, persecution, and perhaps a violent death. Can you consent to all this, for the sake of him who left his heavenly home, and died for her and for you; for the sake of perishing, immortal souls; for the sake of Zion, and the glory of God? Can you consent to all this, in hope of soon meeting your daughter in the world of glory, with the crown of righteousness?*

Her father told him that it was her decision to make. As Anne thought about this decision, she wrote the following note to her friend Lydia Kimball:

> *I feel willing, and expect, if nothing in Providence prevents, to spend my days in this world in heathen lands. Yes, Lydia, I have about come to the determination to give up all my comforts and enjoyments here, sacrifice my affection to relatives and friends, and go where God, in his Providence, shall see fit to place me.*

So in 1813 they left for Burma. They would experience one hardship after another. In 1824 Adoniram was put in prison. He was there for eighteen months. At night his feet were tied up and hoisted up into the air till only his shoulder and head rested on the ground. It was often 110 degrees, and the mosquitoes would eat him alive at night. When he went to prison Anne was pregnant, but she walked two miles every day to plead that Adoniram be released.

After a year in prison, eating rotting food, Adoniram had wasted away. He was dressed in rags and crippled from torture. His daughter, Maria, was born while he was in prison. Anne was as sick and thin as Adoniram. Her milk dried up. Mercifully the jailer actually let Adoniram out of prison each evening so he could take the baby into the village and beg for women to nurse the baby. Eventually Adoniram was released. Not long after that Anne died at thirty-seven from spotted fever. Because of Adoniram and Anne's efforts though, the entire Bible was translated into Burmese. Today there are 3700 congregations that all trace their beginning to when Adoniram and Anne Judson said to God, *"Wherever."* God pointed to Burma and said, *"What about there?"*

Jesus may point to Burma, or he may point across the street.

This week I listened to a story about a family that dates back to an ordinary day more than fifty years ago. It took place in a small town, St. Joseph, Illinois. It was a lazy Sunday afternoon at home for this family. Two men knocked on the door. One man was named Orville Hubbard. Orville used to work in the oil fields. He had minimal education and was just a very normal, ordinary guy. The other guy was named Dick Wolf. Dick met this young family when their wives were in the hospital giving birth at the same time. They asked if they could come in because they wanted to talk to this family for a few minutes about something really important to them. There was not much else to do, and so the husband invited them in. He sat on the couch with his wife as Orville and Dick began to present the gospel. They talked to this family about what it really meant to have a relationship with Jesus

Christ. The couple sat and listened. There is one small, but important detail I don't want to leave out. There was a young boy playing with his trucks on the floor. He was about eight years old. Everyone thought he was just playing with his toys, but that little boy was hanging onto every word. That day changed everything for that family. The next week the mom and dad, along with their young son, gave their lives to Christ and were baptized. Two ordinary men said *"Wherever,"* and Jesus pointed them to this family's house.

I think it's fair to say that I wouldn't be writing this book if they hadn't done that. The couple that answered the door that day I call Grandma and Grandpa. That little eight-year-old boy playing on the floor with his trucks was my dad. So some day in heaven I'm going to thank Orville and Dick for being followers instead of fans. I'm sure they could've found other things to do that day. My guess is they were pretty nervous when they knocked on that door. I'm sure it was uncomfortable. But two men I've never met decided to follow Jesus *wherever*, and they ended up on my grandparents' front porch.

TWELVE

Whatever. *What about That?*

In Luke 9 we read about another fan who wants to be a follower. Once again it appears that this is someone who is ready to commit to following Jesus:

> Still another said, "I will follow you, Lord; but first let me go back and say goodbye to my family" (v. 61).

This fan agrees to follow Jesus, but not right at this moment. First he wants to say goodbye to his family.

I have to say, this seems like a reasonable request. C'mon Jesus, let the guy say goodbye to his mom and pops. But most likely he's asking for more than going home for a quick hug. The cultural practice of saying goodbye to your family if you were to leave the area would have meant numerous farewell parties and could've lasted a period of weeks.

Jesus almost seems annoyed that the man would make such a request.

> Jesus replied, "No one who puts a hand to the plow and looks back is fit for service in the kingdom of God" (v. 62).

Jesus uses an analogy of someone plowing a field, but instead of giving full attention to his work, he looks back. Jesus knows that this man's request reveals where his heart truly lies. It's not that following Jesus isn't important to this man, but following Jesus isn't his top priority. This man, like so many others we've studied, wants to follow Jesus, but not with everything he has. He's not willing to go all-in. There's something else that has his attention, and he keeps looking back.

Many fans say to Jesus, *"I will follow. Anything and everything I have, I give to you."* But Jesus points to what you're hiding behind your back and says, *"What about that?"* For Nicodemus it was his reputation. For the Rich Young Ruler it was his stuff. For this man it was his family relationships that held him back. These men were willing to follow Jesus, but the relationship wasn't exclusive.

Jesus doesn't want followers who have divided affection or split allegiance. And so Jesus points to what you most value and are most concerned about, and says, *"What about that?"*

For Pam, Jesus was asking, "What about food?" For years she had turned to food rather than Jesus as her source of comfort and satisfaction. She finally realized she couldn't call herself a follower of Jesus if she was unwilling to surrender this area of her life to him.

Steve said, "I want to follow Jesus with everything." And Jesus asked, "What about your entertainment choices?" Steve wanted to be a follower of Jesus, but for a long time he kept looking back to television shows and internet sites that filled him with lust. He wanted to follow Jesus, but not with both hands on the plow; he kept looking back.

Jesus said to Stephanie, "What about your kids?" Stephanie called herself a follower of Jesus, but her life didn't revolve around Jesus. Her life revolved around her kids. Her kids were where she found her greatest joy. Her kids were the source of her greatest fears and anxiety.

To Doug, Jesus asked, "What about your money?" Over the years Doug had found his identity and self-worth not in being a follower of Jesus, but in money and the things money could buy. With a downturn in the economy, Doug began to realize that though he said he would follow Jesus, he spent most of his time looking back.

The reason Jesus is so adamant about followers surrendering everything is because the reality is this: the one thing we are most reluctant to give up is the one thing that has the most potential to become a substitute for him. What we're really talking about here is idolatry. When we are supposed to be following Jesus, who is ahead of us, but find ourselves looking behind us, we are revealing that we are substituting something or someone for him.

When we finally surrender that one thing, we discover the satisfaction that comes from following Jesus that was always missing when we were holding something back.

I know there is a reluctance to go all-in and give Jesus anything and everything. We're afraid of what we'll lose. But Jesus says, *"Do you love me? Do you trust me? Then surrender everything and come follow me."* Trading everything we have for all that he offers is the best deal we could ever make. Jim Elliot, the famous missionary who gave his life trying to reach the Auca Indians of Ecuador, once put it this way:

> *He is no fool who gives what he cannot keep to gain that which he cannot lose.*

Psalm 106:19–20 reflects back on the Israelites worshiping a golden image while Moses was on the mountain receiving the Ten Commandments from God. Here's how the psalmist explains what they did:

> The people made a calf at Mount Sinai;
> they bowed before an image made of gold.
> They traded their glorious God
> for a statue of a grass-eating bull (NLT).

That's just not a good trade. But when we hold something back, we are exchanging that which we refuse to surrender for the opportunity to follow Jesus.

Have you exchanged obediently following Jesus for a car that can really handle the corners? Have you exchanged following Jesus for a job that pays really well? Have you exchanged following Jesus for a house that has all the upgrades? Have you exchanged following Jesus for following the stock index? Have you exchanged following Jesus for following your fantasy football league? That's just not a good trade. Understand it's not that any of those things are wrong or sinful in and of themselves, but for too many of us these good things become God things. They have become too important, and they keep us from following Christ with our whole hearts. Augustine referred to these things as "disordered loves." They may very well be legitimate, but they are out of order in our lives.

As a pastor I have performed dozens and dozens of funerals over the years. More often than not, the person who has passed away is not someone I knew. In order to help me speak about the deceased on a more personal level, I invite the family to gather around and share stories and memories of their loved one. They tell me about the person's hobbies and what they were passionate about. These are the ways the person is known and identified. He was an avid golfer. She was a prolific quilt maker. He was a huge sports fan. She was a gifted decorator. He loved a good cigar. She loved Broadway shows. He was a car enthusiast. She was a talented musician. He was a brilliant businessman. She was the most loving mother. He was the most encouraging dad.

I write down the different ways they describe the person who has passed away. But the whole time the person is being remembered and described, I'm praying, *"Please tell me the person loved Jesus. It's great she's an affectionate mom and gifted decorator and a talented musician, but please say she was a follower of Jesus."*

I want you to imagine that when your life is over, instead of being taken directly to heaven, you find yourself sitting alone in a giant movie theater. This isn't exactly how you thought it would happen, and it would be nice if popcorn were provided, but you wait patiently for the show to start. You're not sure what the movie is going to be; you're just hoping that someone other than George Burns or Morgan Freeman will be playing the part of God. The lights are dimmed, and the opening credits of the movie begin to roll. Immediately you realize that you know the cast. Your parents, your spouse, your children, your friends, are all in the movie. But your name receives the top billing. Apparently, you're the star of this film. The title flashes up on the screen: *Fan or Follower: A What-If Story.*

The opening scene of the movie begins to unfold. Initially you recognize the scene as a real-life event, but then it takes a much different direction than what happened in reality. And each scene in the movie begins with something that really happened but has an ending that isn't consistent with what really happened in your life.

The first scene comes on, and it's immediately familiar to you. You're sitting at a table on a first date. As you listen to the dialogue of the movie, you remember the conversation. The person you were on a date with wasn't a Christian, but you had a lot of fun and decided to continue the relationship. You realize this was when you started to turn away from God. It was the beginning of a long season of spiritual dryness. But in this movie, things go differently. You invite the person to church, but your date has no interest. You decide there is no relationship there. Words come up at the bottom of the screen that read: TWO MONTHS LATER. You are in a church service when that same date comes in and sits next to you and says, "I thought I would give this a try."

The next scene you remember well. You are sitting in a travel agency with your spouse, flipping through cruise pamphlets. And you remember what happened; you chose a beautiful Caribbean cruise, and it was awesome. But in the movie things take a different turn. You set down the pamphlet and remember the mission trip that the church was going to be taking around the same time. You ask your spouse if you can talk outside for a minute. You share your crazy idea. On the way home you call the church and you say, "You know, my spouse and I have been talking, and we'd like to go on a mission trip this year with our vacation time." You watch as the movie shows the two of you visiting an orphanage in Guatemala. The two of you serve food to the children, and you watch as you and your spouse sit on either side of a young girl for lunch. There is a jump cut in the movie, and in this scene the two of you are sitting on either side of that little girl, but as the shot widens you realize you're in your home around your own dinner table.

The scenes continue. You see yourself on the job. A person comes by your office. The scene seems vaguely familiar to you. You recognize this person, but you can't quite place their name. However, you do remember they were one of those high-maintenance people, and you had established some boundaries early on so you wouldn't constantly have to hear about their problems. But in this movie things go differently. You sit down with them, and you listen to them. Then you say, "Can I pray for you?"

The scene changes. You know this one very well. You and your spouse are watching the news. You always did this. It was a nightly ritual. A little news followed by a late-night talk show. But in this movie things go differently. You watch as you turn the TV off and the two of you get on your knees beside the bed. You interlock fingers, and you begin to pray. As you watch this movie you notice that it's not just the scenes that are different in your alternative life as a follower. You are different. There is a joy and a soul satisfaction that comes when we follow Jesus with our whole hearts, and it can't be found anywhere else.

What are the scenes that would unfold differently in your life if you were a follower instead of a fan? What would your life look like if you followed Jesus completely? No excuses. Wherever. Whatever.

> The eyes of the LORD search the whole earth in order to strengthen those whose hearts are fully committed to him.
>
> 2 CHRONICLES 16:9